*1944 Diary*

# 1944

## DIARY

*Hans Keilson*

TRANSLATED FROM THE GERMAN BY
DAMION SEARLS

FARRAR, STRAUS AND GIROUX   NEW YORK

Farrar, Straus and Giroux
18 West 18th Street, New York 10011

Printed in the United States of America
Originally published in German in 2014 by S. Fischer, Germany, as *Tagebuch 1944*
English translation published in the United States by Farrar, Straus and Giroux
First American edition, 2017

Library of Congress Cataloging-in-Publication Data
Names: Keilson, Hans, 1909–2011, author.
Title: 1944 diary / Hans Keilson ; translated from the German by Damion Searls.
Other titles: Tagebuch 1944. English
Description: First American edition. | New York : Farrar, Straus and Giroux, 2017. |
    "Originally published in German in 2014 by S. Fischer, Germany, as Tagebuch
    1944" — Title page verso.
Identifiers: LCCN 2016045036 | ISBN 9780374535599 (hardback) |
    ISBN 9780374713898 (e-book)
Subjects: LCSH: Keilson, Hans, 1909–2011—Diaries. | Authors, German—20th
    century—Diaries. | Jews, German—Netherlands—Diaries. | World War,
    1939–1945—Netherlands—Delft. | World War, 1939–1945—Underground
    movements—Netherlands. | World War, 1939–1945—Personal narratives,
    Jewish. | World War, 1939–1945—Personal narratives, Dutch. | Netherlands—
    History—German occupation, 1940–1945. | Sonnets, German. | BISAC:
    BIOGRAPHY & AUTOBIOGRAPHY / Personal Memoirs. | HISTORY /
    Jewish. | HISTORY / Holocaust.
Classification: LCC PT2621.E24 Z4613 2017 | DDC 833/.912 [B] —dc23
LC record available at https://lccn.loc.gov/2016045036

Designed by Abby Kagan

Our books may be purchased in bulk for promotional, educational, or business
use. Please contact your local bookseller or the Macmillan Corporate and
Premium Sales Department at 1-800-221-7945, extension 5442, or by e-mail at
MacmillanSpecialMarkets@macmillan.com.

www.fsgbooks.com
www.twitter.com/fsgbooks • www.facebook.com/fsgbooks

10  9  8  7  6  5  4  3  2  1

# CONTENTS

Hans Keilson's *1944 Diary*, written while he was in hiding from the Nazis in the Dutch city of Delft, is a unique document.

Its most obvious counterpart is the diary of another German-born Jew in the Netherlands during World War II. Anne Frank. But they were very different people—Keilson a grown man and father, largely free to walk the streets and travel throughout the country; Frank, of course, never reaching adulthood, betrayed and arrested on August 4, 1944. Still, Keilson's diary is an immensely revealing complement to Frank's diary, helping show how much of Frank's wartime experience was the product of its time and place and how much was particular to her.

And Hanna Sanders, Keilson's lover, who plays such a large role in his diary and an even larger role in the mental and spiritual struggles lying behind it, was only seven years older than Anne Frank—a kind of alternate-reality smart, curious, sensitive, literary young Jewish woman in Nazi-occupied Holland. We see Sanders only through Keilson's eyes, but he was too good a writer and observer for her own personality not to shine through, especially in the outpouring of poems he wrote for her and about her experiences, such as the destruction of her home during the bombing of Rotterdam.

Keilson was not just any writer. His novel *Comedy in a Minor Key*, published in 1947, was widely recognized as a masterpiece when it was finally translated into English in 2010. It is about a Jew in hiding in Delft who dies of natural causes, and now what are his hosts supposed to do with the body without getting caught? The emotional center of the novel is not the man in hiding, as one might expect from an author in hiding himself, but instead the ordinary people around him, doing their best in a dark time. The diary reveals that he wrote the novel between April and June 1944, about a real incident. Hanna Sanders translated it into Dutch.

Few such works of Chekhovian sympathy are written in such pressurized circumstances, and none that I know of are accompanied by a document like this diary—a kind of spiritual X-ray of the mind and heart behind the art. (Literature, Keilson remarks at one point, "can only be understood starting out from the person writing it.") The closest analogy I can think of is the other most famous book written in Dutch, besides Frank's: the letters of Vincent van Gogh. Keilson was writing for himself, and unlike the painter's letters, the diary is often terse and cryptic, leaving out information a reader would need to understand quite what is going on. But both vividly bring to life their authors' doubts about how to possibly pursue their true calling. In 1944, even while writing *Comedy* and the dozens of sonnets to Hanna, Keilson was not sure he was cut out to be a writer at all. The diary is not a writer's notebook; it shows someone stepping back to struggle with what it might mean to be a writer, and a human being.

Perhaps the greatest surprise of *1944 Diary* is that it is less about Keilson's day-to-day life and survival than about the moral and artistic existence he was struggling to create for himself. There are a couple of show-stopping set pieces in the book—an encounter with a Dutch pastor sick of having to help Jews; a long entry written in pencil, in real time, during a Nazi roundup in the neighborhood. But as a whole it is mostly about his affair with Hanna, his poems, his notes on reading Kafka, Rilke, Céline, Baudelaire, Buber, and others. News of the Allied reconquest of the Netherlands, the fall of Nazi Germany, appears only in passing. Wartime events, he writes, "however much they grip me, are no longer my real life": what's real is "the human being, the poem, people together." This is why the poems are included in *1944 Diary*: they are not just a crucial record of Keilson's experience, they *are* the core of his experience.

The diary and sonnets to Hanna are a testament to finding one's way amid horrors and conflicts of all kinds. Human struggles can outweigh even the Holocaust, world war, the Dutch Hunger Winter. When Keilson called 1944 "the most critical year in my life," he meant its inner significance. As he would write near the diary's end: "If you push and push you eventually force a way to your center."

Hans Alex Keilson was born in 1909, in a town in eastern Germany near Poland. In 1933, he was twenty-three years old and leading a busy life in Berlin: studying medicine, qualifying as a state-certified swimming and gymnastics instructor, playing trumpet in a jazz band at night, helping support his parents after his father's store had gone out of business, and awaiting publication of his first novel, the autobiographical *Life Goes On*, which would be the last novel by a Jewish writer published by Fischer Verlag before the war. Through Fischer, he met literary luminaries such as Bertolt Brecht, Alfred Döblin, and Franz Hessel.

One night, at a classmate's party, he met Gertrud Manz, who had already been married and divorced and had a child, born in 1922. They stayed at the party until four in the morning, then walked through the streets of Berlin, sat down on a bench, and continued talking until dawn. Keilson would much later describe her appeal as follows: "She was an adult woman I could talk to as an adult man and who treated me as such. This was actually the first time in my life that I felt taken seriously by a woman, socially speaking." She was "seven years older than me and opened up new perspectives; she was a completely new kind of person in my experience. Psychoanalytical, without having herself been analyzed; in contact with doctors, lawyers, psychologists; used to dealing with Jewish people. She was different, she lived differently, and she knew what was happening and what was going to happen."

And so, in 1936, the Catholic Gertrud convinced the Jewish Hans to flee Germany. They traveled to the Netherlands as "tourists," with practically no money, and stayed first in Amsterdam, soon afterward at various addresses in nearby Naarden, where a relative of Keilson's worked at the residence-permit office and could help them. Keilson mastered Dutch and was able to find work as a swimming and gym teacher, editorial assistant, and counselor in schools and other institutions. He and Gertrud lived in different houses on the same street. They had a stillborn son in 1940; their daughter, Barbara, was born in 1941, nineteen years after Gertrud's first child. Gertrud pretended that the father was a German soldier, to protect Barbara and herself.

The Germans had conquered the Netherlands in May 1940. Despite the antiauthoritarian character of the people and the resistance activity of many of the Dutch, the Netherlands proved dangerous indeed to the Jews: the country would eventually be known as the Holocaust's "Poland of the West," with the highest proportion in any nation of Jews turned in, Jews murdered, non-Jews serving in the German war machine. By early 1941, the 160,000 Jews in the country, 137,000 of them Dutch, were required to register at the "Central Jewish Emigration Bureau," resulting in their deportation via Westerbork transit camp; of the more than 101,000 Jews deported, barely 6,000 survived. The first razzias or roundups of Jews came in February 1941; the yellow star for Jews was introduced in May 1942. Gertrud and Hans had managed to get Hans's parents out of Germany in 1938, but in April 1943 his parents were taken to Westerbork and, instead of being allowed to emigrate to Palestine as promised, sent to Auschwitz.

Keilson went underground himself in the spring of 1943, without Gertrud and Barbara. (In Dutch, the metaphor is "underwater": to go into hiding is *duiken*, "to dive.") From April 10 until September 7, he stayed with Henk Fontein, a friend from his time in Naarden and the adjacent village of Bussum—Fontein was former principal of the Bussum Montessori School and now the director of a psychiatric clinic and institution for youths with behavior problems in Rekken, a small village on the eastern edge of the Netherlands about half a mile from Germany.

In September 1943, after a new law was passed mandating that everyone had to live in the province where their passport was issued, Keilson decided to move back west from Rekken. He took the train to Delft, where he had been offered housing with another Dutchman he had met in Naarden, Leo Rientsma. As Keilson would later describe him: "A tall, skinny man with a duck's bill face, extraordinarily composed and able to swiftly see through critical situations, endowed with tact and natural wit."

Leo Rientsma, his wife Suus (Suzanna), and their two daughters, Lieske (Lies) and Hannie (Hanna), lived at Wallerstraat 3 in Delft. Leo was a member of a small resistance group that specialized in forging documents; he was horrified to see Keilson's amateurish papers, which any routine inspection would have caught. With a brand-new passport in the name of Dr. Johannes Gerrit van der Linden, born in Semarang, Dutch East Indies, Keilson lived with the Rientsmas for more than a year, officially as a subletter and tutor for the two daughters.

Other Jews in hiding stayed with the Rientsmas for short periods, along with one other long-term refugee, Corrie Groenteman, officially their maid. The neighbors at Wallerstraat 5, the van der Leks, were also in the know—there was a secret passageway from one attic to the next in case of emergency. And some ten minutes away on foot, at Tak van Poortvlietstraat 20, lived two of Rientsma's fellow resistance members, Arie Bakker and his wife, Evy. Their house contained the workshop where documents were forged, including Hans Keilson's passport, using materials Leo Rientsma obtained in secret from a factory where he worked as a chemical engineer. The Bakkers also housed Jews in hiding, including a twenty-two-year-old woman whose father had been the head of the Jewish community in Rotterdam before the war: Hanna Sanders.

With his perfect Dutch and perfect fake ID, "Dr. van der Linden" was free to move about the country. "The new passport gave me such a strong sense of security that I almost forgot my old identity," Keilson later wrote. His work in the resistance consisted of giving psychological counseling to children and teenagers in hiding throughout Holland—in those circumstances, a fed-up teenager threatening to break the house rules could be life-threatening—before returning to Delft and his own life in hiding.

The diary was closely written in pale blue ink on forty-one and a half folio pages, later bound by hand. He wrote it in German, as he did his novels and the poems to Hanna, though here the German is marked by occasional phrases in Dutch and numerous Dutchisms. The Dutch edition of the diary, *Dagboek 1944*, was often useful for interpreting difficult parts of the text and has a different set of notes than the German edition; I consulted it throughout my translation. All footnotes in the text are mine, many of them translated or adapted from the German or Dutch notes, both by Marita Keilson-Lauritz. I am also grateful to Marita for thoroughly reviewing my translation and clearing up many obscure passages.

Many paragraph breaks have been added to the translation, since Keilson omitted them wherever possible to save space, and German tends to be written in longer paragraphs anyway. Section breaks have been added for the English reader as well, to indicate or provide pauses in the narrative.

The diary opens in early 1944. Hans Keilson is thirty-four years old.

—Damion Searls

PEOPLE

**JOHANNES GERRIT VAN DER LINDEN:** Hans Keilson's false identity.

**GERTRUD MANZ** (1901–69): Keilson's wife, although technically they are not yet married in 1944; living in Naarden.

**DADAUT:** Keilson's pet name for Gertrud.

**BARBARA** (b. 1941): Keilson and Gertrud's child.

**HANNA SANDERS** (1921–2008): Keilson's lover, in hiding with the Bakkers.

**LEO RIENTSMA** (1899–1985) and **SUUS (SUZANNA) RIENTSMA**, née Warsen (1898–1972): The Dutch couple whose house at Wallerstraat 3 Keilson is living in.

**LIESKE** or **LIES** (b. 1933) and **HANNIE** or **HANNA** (b. 1935): The Rientsma daughters.

**ARIE BAKKER** (1914–92) and **EVY BAKKER**, née Beer (1910–81): Two of the Rientsmas' fellow resistance members, whose house at Tak van Poortvlietstraat 20 contains a workshop where documents are forged, including Hans Keilson's passport. Hanna Sanders is in hiding there.

**EMMA BEER,** née Longo (1882–1960): Evy Bakker's Italian mother, a poetry aficionado.

**ROSALINA "CORRIE" GROENTEMAN,** née Speijer (1902–87): The other Jew in hiding at the Rientsmas' for an extended period, officially their maid. Her children Esther (b. 1923) and Abraham or Bram (b. 1924) are rounded up in Amsterdam in 1942 and killed at Auschwitz; her younger daughter, Sonja (b. 1938), survives.

**CORA** and **JAN VAN DER LEK:** The Rientsmas' neighbors at Wallerstraat 5, with attics connecting through a secret door. Jan is a colleague of Leo Rienstma's at the yeast factory. He plays the flute, she the piano. Their son is also named Bram, like Corrie Groenteman's.

The **VAN OYENS:** Friends of the van der Leks, living on the upper floor of Wallerstraat 5 after being evacuated from The Hague. Keilson hears their daughter, Hanneke, playing the piano.


**JOOP ANDRIESSE:** Jewish member of the resistance staying briefly with the Rientsmas; Keilson attends his wedding to Sofie "Fiet" Hes.

**EVERT:** Probably Andriesse, whose fake ID bears the name Evert Jonker.

**CAS EMMER** (1909–2005): Keilson's oldest Dutch friend

and his personal physician for decades after the war. Together with Keilson, Emmer formed a kind of reading group with figures including Jan Thomassen, Rudi Buys, and the poet Jef Last.

JAN THOMASSEN (1908–51): Friend of Keilson's and Emmer's. He worked as Prince Bernhard's personal secretary after the war, and his brother Wim Thomassen was mayor of Rotterdam from 1965 to 1974.

RUDI: W. R. van Brakell Buys (1905–78), Anglicist, philosopher, and rector of a theosophical school in Naarden after 1938.

EVERWIJN VERSCHUYL (1903–97): Surgeon in Delft and mentor for Keilson; he lets Keilson assist him as a doctor.

CORRIE HARTONG (1906–91): A famous Dutch dancer and choreographer, mentioned several times in the diary, with her name spelled in different ways.


Other people mentioned only once are identified in the footnotes; names not annotated are of people who remain unidentified.

*Diary*

Conscience—or conflict? What are the motives driving me: self-justification or reflection? Defense or acknowledgment. Guilt or atonement, crime or punishment. Both. I have reached the point where I can drop my disguise. Finally. I am grateful to—yes, to whom? The first time I kept a kind of personal diary was as a boy, before my bar mitzvah. It was on my father's letterhead with his business and bank account information on the sheets of paper. The entries recorded my religious feelings.[1] Later, when I began to write, I burned it. I thought it was unnecessary, my writing seemed to be "confession" and record enough.

Last summer, when my tooth bled for eight hours until I fainted, I understood Hebbel's diary.[2] I understood for

1. Keilson would later be more specific: these "feelings" were his doubts, his loss of faith. See chapter 3 of his memoir, *Da steht mein Haus*, drafted in the 1990s and edited and published in 2011. An English translation has been published only in Australia, as *There Stands My House*. Cited below as *My House*.

2. The German writer Friedrich Hebbel (1813–63) began his famous diary in 1835, in the throes of a love affair.

the first time (!) that writing does not make a diary unnecessary—it requires a diary, presupposes it. The issue is an art that comes only from "life"—a courage to strive for truth. Nothing else. "Art is autonomous," as Corrie Hartoog said? More on that later.

The burning desire to keep a diary came over me at home, with Gertrud and the child.

**Friday, March 3rd, '44.**   German soldiers sitting in the streetcar when I got on. A scene I know all too well! But something struck me about these soldiers. Strangely chiseled faces—made me think of Austria at first, Styria or Carinthia. They weren't Prussians, that was obvious. Suddenly they started talking: a Slavic language. I took a closer look and saw a round patch pinned on their left arms with the inscription: Idel-Ural, and below it: Tatar Legion. Russians! In German uniforms! The most biting comedy I have ever seen, there on my way to The Hague. Either Russian prisoners, or deserters, stuck into German uniforms to defend Europe . . . against whom? The twilight of power politics.

Slavically chiseled faces. Some peasants, some middle class. One of them stood up to give his seat to a lady and squeezed in with his comrades on the opposite bench even though there was only room for two. They talked with each other not in the clipped, staccato, insolent melody that the Germans have decided to adopt, but gently, warm and human like boys—comradely, brotherly even. The way Tolstoy's Russians must talk to each other, and only they can. They'll get their heads chopped off if the English or Americans catch them, because they're traitors, or poor devils who couldn't stand prisoner's food any longer and moved up to soldier's rations. They'll hang them—and maybe that's what they deserve. But these are people, human faces, not hardened brutes. Russians in German uniforms with swastikas.

I remember the Russian prisoners from the last war. They stood behind my father and me in synagogue. I slid down the bench toward them and peeked in their prayer books. They were Russians but they understood Hebrew, they were praying in Hebrew. So then they weren't foreigners? Yes, yes they were, and to me the combination of Russian and Hebrew became the epitome of foreignness.

**Sunday, 5th.** No fear. No more fear of looking at myself in the mirror. No more whitewashing. I'm saying what I say to myself in secret. The blank sheet of paper's power to inhibit the writing and thinking process has been overcome. I will write down my thoughts and experiences. My conscience is not turned off, but it is no longer afraid of expressing itself. Ethical conflict? Infidelity. Or truth even in going astray, no metaphysical pretenses? I haven't played the role that my "profession" should have made me play vis-à-vis Hanna.[3] I didn't present myself as superior. The bliss of being subordinate. Finally, for once, the grace of inferiority. And no secrecy.

I can't tell Gertrud anything. "Please, no problems, not now," she said last time. This determines my attitude. My poems will tell her the whole story someday. What sustains me is a land I have longed to live in but have never known. No poetic circumlocutions, my dear Hans: longed to live *and write* in. I have never felt it inside me so deeply, so ardently. Does a daemon have me in its grip? But I crouch down only so that I can pull him into this circle of mine on the other side—to subdue him, to create. Things change. I will come out of this time a different person. Ecstasy! How I long for it—a longing left over from last summer when I fainted—maybe so that it will guide my choice.

It's not just being everything to someone, to Hanna, I'm sure she has her problems with me anyway. It was our almost total lack of a past when we came together, although everyone has a past with other people. She is a mirror to me like no one has ever been before. I will take care it doesn't get cracked, doesn't cloud over.

**Monday. 3/6.** Feel a stronger need to write this diary. What is love? More than just a local itch and then

3. His "profession" as a counselor to young people in hiding.

6

scratching it. Had I forgotten this most basic rule of love, that God is in the lover? Not only in the beloved. I couldn't stand it anymore, being the "beloved," being worshipped. It flattered my vanity too much. I was afraid it was all just vanity. Someone, a girl, in love but she can't be yet, she doesn't know love. Until I decided to dare to take the step I had already taken in my imagination. If only I didn't feel like I was destroying what I had previously built up in her. A premonition that could only be grasped or formulated mystically, = fear. But I took the step, against my vanity, and then I wasn't in the superior position after all. The nights we spent together. She came to me as a girl, and remained one. Her nature made sure of that. I let go of my fear of the consequences, my fear of surprises. My conscience built up crime and punishment where they never actually, causally existed. Complete abandon, the stammering, the whispering, as a sign of a breath that is all a person has left.

Never before has anyone lain in my arms like that. Was I ever that close to God, ever, as I was then, in that total surrender? The girl's complete loss of self. The safety and security of the nothingness she came to me with. Knowing that there was at the same time something to protect her. Trusting me not to deceive her. She feels the conflict and is very gentle, restrained. The poems I wrote for her are the toll I paid. What was it Achterberg said when Tammenons Bakker asked aren't you sorry?[4] *But I've written five poems!* Moral insanity?[5] Well, so far I've written nine. Conscience does function as more than just a mechanism for regret and guilty feelings, after all.

Read Martin Buber. *The Struggle for Israel.* His speech to the Christian missionaries to the Jews is magnificent: Jewish Foci.[6] A true critique of Christianity. I've seen a lot of perfect examples myself, visiting pastors. His essay on Mombert is masterful too.[7] And that he spoke up in the Zionist Congress.— When I read the speech, I had the feeling that here was someone

---

4. Gerrit Achterberg (1905–62), one of the most important Dutch poets of the twentieth century, spent several years in a psychiatric prison for shooting and killing his landlady (with whom he may have had a relationship) and seriously wounding her sixteen-year-old daughter (with whom he wanted to have a relationship). Keilson, a great admirer of Achterberg's poetry, met him in 1941 and saw him many times while he was in hiding in Rekken in the home of Henk Fontein, the director of Achterberg's hospital; the Keilson-Achterberg correspondence has been published (*Maandblad Geestelijke Volksgezondheid* 58 [2003]: 783–803). S. P. Tammenons Bakker was one of Achterberg's psychiatrists.

5. In English in the original.

6. "Two Foci of the Jewish Soul," in English in *Israel and the World: Essays in a Time of Crisis*; originally in *Kampf um Israel: Reden und Schriften, 1921–1932* (*The Struggle for Israel: Speeches and Writings*), which Keilson owned.

7. Expressionist poet Alfred Mombert (1872–1942); Buber's essay "Alfred Mombert," from 1922.

speaking who knew he wasn't being heard. It sounds uncertain, he bases his argument on his own life, bears witness— A tragic constellation. He must have felt this uncertainty himself, his not entirely equal position. You can sense it: only the ethos or insight of an unpolitical person can drive one to politics. But it *isn't* an equal position, there are too many money changers. With slicker hands.

Kafka, the bleak light of his burning despair. His artistic skill often conceals it. But his wound is deeper than Kierkegaard's. I understand him more than I used to. Why didn't I buy his books before? Something my father said, when I wanted to go to the theater to see Kortner as Shylock:[8] "There'll be time for that later." I've been living for years in that "later." Waiting. That's why my "here and now" is often so hopeless.

Hanna wrote that she feels like love wears a person out. Poor thing, she doesn't see that when something is lost, something new comes into being. She sees only the wearing down, not the filling up. Lack of concentration. A girl with the uncertainty of an intellectual who has felt the ground pulled out from under his feet. Or is it something else. She refuses to say the word, so as to avoid conflict. She holds back. I know I'll lose you, she

8. The Jewish actor Fritz Kortner (1892–1970) played Shylock in Shakespeare's *The Merchant of Venice* several times in Berlin, the first in 1923.

wrote. A despair that isn't clear yet. But I'm losing too. Which one of us is losing more? The one who's playing for higher stakes. Only who's that? For all my deep and genuine respect for her, I definitely feel like I'm the one playing for higher stakes. But is that just the whispering of the devil?

Read a lot of Baudelaire. Amazing poems. The introduction by Gautier, with the apology for decadence, is even more amazing.[9] Baudelaire, as a son of the church, believed in Hell and damnation. Was attracted and repelled by it at the same time. Great courage. Goethe would have shied away, preferring to stick to the middle. What amazes me is the absence of any messianic pathos as he sanctifies "evil" with his poems. His clear-sighted look at the brokenness, the damned state of human existence, all the while without a "will to heal." His ahistorical perspective is almost inhuman in its humanity.

Being content in an unredeemed state! That is probably the final consequence of Christianity, which defines its redemption historically, referring to a specific moment in time—but which also gives daily proof of daily unredemption. Actually, Baudelaire *is* the final consequence of Christianity.

The conversation with Corrie Hartoog was about my not letting a poem, for example a Baudelaire poem,

9. The Romantic poet Théophile Gautier introduced the 1868 edition of Baudelaire's *Les Fleurs du Mal* (*Flowers of Evil*).

be what it is—instead I want to know more. A kind of curiosity drives me to take in the whole background behind a poem; this background is sealed inside Baudelaire himself. The more I immerse myself in his work, his character, his life, the more capacious my experience of the poem becomes. The immediate experience Baudelaire must have had when he wrote the poem is communicated to me. Only when art emerges from a person's life does it matter to me; the so-called autonomous laws of art, understood as formal problems, are important only as a result of that. C.H. denied this and wanted to present it as a scientific, unartistic viewpoint of mine. It seemed like everything she said was about trying to hold my scientific attitude against me. Meanwhile I had already explicitly said the same thing about her, in a letter. Still, she's wrong. Even a poem can only be understood starting out from the person writing it. There's no other way. Not as the expression of a mood, of feelings, but as the expression of an encounter: a way of being and conducting oneself, an experience of life. That is exactly what Rilke meant when he described poems as experiences. Experiences embody ways of being, which we have to reveal completely in order to grasp a given experience as the expression of lived life. Is that unartistic? Just because it is also intellectual? It is thought *and* lived. Thought of as a living thing, lived as something thought.

The idea of mercy, as Christianity understands it,

displaces all action onto God. The person merely waits. Of course that's true. But at the same time the human being is a partner in the conversation, someone who can start or stop on their own. In any case, someone in whom God's creative intentions have power too. More power than original sin has.

Corri Hartog talked about the person being an "instrument." I said a person was more than just that. My response was clumsy and labored, as I so often am. Something about her irritated me. In the good sense— not annoyed me, but in the sense that I was engaged by more than what she was saying. From what depths was she speaking, actually? I haven't yet plumbed her depths.

Maybe the human being is redeemed after all, "after all"—not by Christ—but in his own spirit, in the creative element he feels working within him. A breath of air from another world, when he surpasses his own limits and becomes one with his transcendence, for a few seconds, in a moment made holy. But he is damned in the world, in doing what must be done. It would be a terrible break, a battle never to be ended, traceable back to the inner battle of God within himself.

Sickness—is that the ultimate cause of creative madness?

**Monday. Evening.**
Talked to Hanna. "After all, I don't have any right to you," she said. And yet such closeness while we talked,

full of deep understanding. "Do you only do things for pedagogical reasons?" she said. I tried to explain my motives. And in doing so laid out part of my conflict. She listened happily. I was shocked to realize how deeply I was drawn to her. "Affinity" I called it—kindred spirits. A girl you are talking to has a gaze rising up out of mysterious depths, looking into a mysterious distance. Thinking it over, seeking. This look made a different face shine through her features.

Letter from Gertrud. Very sad, she's not well. I understand her deeply. She is alone, I start to cry when I think about her. It is she who is suffering from my conflict. I am anything but kind to her. I hate myself, hate my resentment. And, even more, my earlier fear that kept me from seeing the truth. We don't go together. We are completely different types, despite our deep affinities. I'm still shuddering, she is not calm and self-possessed enough. Nervous. And doesn't understand men. Too primitive. So I have nothing but criticisms? No, no, when I reread "The Dreamer"[10] I know that I wrote that poem at my limits.

10. In the summer of 1943, Keilson wrote "To a Dreamer," a long (350-line) blank-verse poem to Gertrud, addressing her as the kind of ancient seer whose dreams foretell the future, from the fireball engulfing her country to the birth and death of her own child. In the dreamer's last vision, referred to several times later in the diary, she is alone at sea and witnesses an apocalyptic night finally breaking with the light of dawn. "Look, day has

I don't want to be paralyzed anymore, the way I am when I'm with her. But I am. I can't work, and when I go away I become productive. Is our little Barbara the price I'll have to pay to buy my freedom from her? Constant thoughts of separation. We never had a silent mutual understanding. I need it so much. Her ears.[11] Oh, Dadaut[12]—I constantly see her fearful face looking at me. Was your father right after all, when he said I would leave you? If only you weren't so stubborn, this hardheadedness I've almost shattered against.

Since I stopped living at home I've been in a rush of productivity like I've never known. And yet I owe so much to Gertrud. She set everything in motion. Sexually we go together well, very well. I love her body grown heavy, it is like a home to me. When I'm in bed with her I feel at home. But sex life isn't what ultimately matters most in a marriage. I don't know how this all will end.

The fact that I can speak softly to Hanna, that she can hear me when I whisper—it means so much, and at the same time it's so petty. It's not something I need . . .

---

come!" she cries. Then another voice speaks: "Something, though, remains for you." A black strip of darkness wafts down from the sky, over her shoulder, into her hand. "So the dream ended, the final one you've dreamed. / What will it be? You ask, and wait, atremble / for the gift."

11. Gertrud was very hard of hearing; Keilson couldn't whisper with her, as he mentions again later in this entry.

12. Keilson's pet name for Gertrud; significance unknown.

and yet I do, I miss it so much with Gertrud. When you talk louder things become harder, they move to another level. Usually a lower one.

**Wednesday. 3/8.**   Gertrud came over unexpectedly. Looked bad. "I'm falling apart, I'm dying," she wrote. Violent conflict in me, between deepest affinity and still deepest estrangement. At first, a purely negative situation, through unwillingness. Avoided the catastrophe. By not doing anything, lying there, apparently waiting— she came round and became affectionate. Intimate. Hanna recedes into the background. Along with the poems, and everything else. Just sensual reality—which I seek out but then often run away from. In the afternoon, Gertrud said: "I think you're so crude because you save up your finer feelings for your poems." Finally! I agreed. "I can accept that, as long as you don't put me down." (Her inability to read a situation.) But there it is. Gave her the poem after Leopardi:[13] I've moved beyond *spyt*,[14] I said. I feel like Gertrud knows what's happening. Not from any details, but from "knowledge without experience." Her sickness. Is it killing her? This causal connection—magical, not logical—I'm finally breaking it.

13. Keilson's poem "To Death (after Leopardi)." Keilson later recalled reading poems by the Italian poet Giacomo Leopardi (1798–1837) in Delft with Hanna, but it may have been with Evy Bakker's mother, Mrs. Beer, an Italian.
14. Dutch: "regret."

It constitutes my unfreedom. My outbursts. Rage against hidden powers!

Read Kafka. Moved to tears by lines from "The Great Wall of China": "We sit dreaming at the window and wait for that message." Or: "From the thunder-clouds that have long since passed flashes no more lightning!" Reminds me of A. Roland Holst, "Winter by the Lake."[15] *Uit welk oud vergeetboek*—. Almost exactly the same, down to the sentence rhythm. The burden of not being able to believe, along with a mythical knowledge of the possibility of belief. That's how the possibility of healing is wasted. "Heil H."!—this too has to be understood as coming from a squandered desire for healing. But every concretization is at the same time a blasphemy. And this particular gentleman doesn't know anything about Kafka—otherwise he would have been more careful. Familiarity with literature is useful for politicians. Just ask the French, they know that.

Evening. When I'm with Gertrud, I don't understand what connects me to Hanna. When I'm with Hanna, Gertrud seems very far away. But both times, it's "I."

15. Well-known cycle of poems (1937) by the Dutch poet Adriaan Roland Holst (1888–1976); Keilson quotes the opening line of the first poem in Part III: "From which old book of forgetting / Do the healing words / Eddy over us like a curse?" These words of healing are, in German, words of *Heil*, which also means "Hail!"; *Heil Hitler!* means "Hail Hitler," but is also a homonym for "Heal, Hitler!" Keilson picks up on the resonance just below.

Amazing, this "I" that both these women apparently value—as a unity. Still, I have to recognize both signatures as valid. This recognizing "I" is the third setting. That's the one you have to be careful of.—

The autonomy of the artist? Gautier's introduction to Baudelaire, *l'art pour l'art*. Art as an "eccentric" phenomenon? In the end, the artist too is just one form of life among others, like the soldier, the whore, the worker, etc. Every one of these forms must have its own "autonomy." Play by its own rules, the way soccer has different rules than tennis. Ultimately, it's like with the pagans, who saw another new god behind every phenomenon. Monotheism put an end to that. The autonomy of the artist is "heathen." Being an artist is likewise one form of existence among others; behind it there is always "the" living human being. The various forms are diverse because people are diverse, e.g. Whore A is a different form of life than Whore B. But actually that's not true. What is true? Sink or swim. Swim *and* sink. That's what life is for the living! Whore *and* artist—one for money, the other for art!! A typical attitude for a bourgeois person with a nice front parlor. But the paradox is: This nice parlor was necessary for the creation of a *Fleurs du Mal* too. Baudelaire's confusion of life with the rules of the game.

My impatience and excitability are worse than before. Does that mean something has been stirred up, or that something new is being created? More advanced technology only makes it harder to deal with the world. Increasing outrage, unjust rage, dissatisfaction—and boredom, like I've never felt. Blessed floating in inaction! Heidegger comes to mind.— A modern way of committing and concealing crimes: thinking ontologically.

Hanna thought that "To Death" was *by* Leopardi, and thought it was wonderful. She said she had a feeling I was tricking her. I don't like the poem as much. Only the experience it grew out of remains. In a train while crossing a bridge I felt like we were falling into the water—and I did nothing. I shrank into my corner and felt blissful. I wouldn't do a thing. I felt myself doing nothing, just slowly disappearing. The same feeling as last summer, when I fainted. I'd often longed for that same rush. And now I had it, crossing over the water in a train. That's how the first line came to me.[16]

Buber says: Culture is an epiphenomenon. You can't aim for culture, it arises as a by-product of a life process. Art is the same: The life must be—and then there can be art. But that means there is no autonomy. QED.

Mombert, in Buber interpretation: The intellect is the creative element. (Klages!!!)[17] The human being as

16. The poem begins: "Slowly, Death is becoming my friend. / Already it's dawning in my blood, / free of tears I see his image reflected / in the cool waters."

17. German Nietzschean philosopher and psychologist Ludwig Klages (1872–1956), widely read and influential in the early twentieth century, not least as the inventor of modern handwriting

the peer of God. Experiencing the self equals eternal creation—art—autonomous? The unity is not given, it must be generated in the person. Finally: The person as not only an instrument, mercy—the person as the peer of creation. Prometheus, how much bolder than Christ! The "I" is not a person, but an Aeon of Creation.[18]

---

analysis (*Handwriting and Character* [1917]; see, e.g., Walter Benjamin's essays "Review of the Mendelssohns' *Der Mensch in der Handschrift* [*Man in His Handwriting*]" [1928] and "Graphology Old and New" [1930] and other references to Klages in Benjamin's *Selected Writings*). Gertrud would have known and studied Klages's graphological works. In his multivolume treatise *The Intellect as Adversary of the Soul* (1929–33), Klages argued and lamented that the rational intellect had destroyed the original unity of body and soul—ideas welcomed into Nazi ideology, whose antisemitism Klages also shared.

18. A Gnostic Christian and kabbalistic Jewish mystical concept: the Aeons were the semi-personified Divine Forces, varying in number in the different systems. For instance, in the twelfth-century *Bahir*, the mystical work that brought Gnostic elements into the kabbalah, God prior to all creation established an "aeon of creation," the primordial time to which, at the redemption, everything returns.

The three-step process Keilson describes next has certain affinities with the related kabbalistic idea, propounded by Isaac Luria (1534–72), that the Infinite first had to withdraw into itself, in an act of *tzimtzum* (contraction, concealment, concentration), in order to make room for the creation of the universe. A new beam of light from the original Infinite Light then shone into the (nonspatial) "empty vessels" of the resulting vacuum, becoming the source for all subsequent creation while also shattering the vessels, which then had to be restored or repaired. This mythical,

I. Memory (recollecting). II. Absorption. III. Encounter. (I and Thou!) The world is enacted! Our action follows from this recognition, not as the need to persevere but as a need for eternal procreation and bringing to completion. The history of the human spirit is one with the world spirit. So, then, can you talk about fate as the mystery of the beginning and the mystery of the end, in which a people, self-fathering, must become itself? Jewish existence as "human existence" par excellence!

**Monday. 13th.**    At Arie and Evy's again.[19] Again *het samenzyn met het meisje van 16 jaar* (Achterberg).[20] This evening, while I was out for a walk, the line suddenly came to me: *afspraak buiten de wet.* The first time I read that line, it shot through me like an experience I had yet to undergo. When I saw Achterberg, he asked me what I thought of those four or five poems. I hadn't read them yet, I had only heard that they existed. He told me

---

cosmological process—withdrawal and exile followed by a need for redemption—resonated with many aspects of Jewish thought and Jewish history.

19. The Bakkers, Hanna's hosts at Tak van Poortvlietstraat 20.

20. "Being with a sixteen-year-old girl," from Gerrit Achterberg's poem cycle "Sixteen," slightly misquoted from memory. (Hanna was twenty-two, not sixteen.) The cycle originally had four poems but would soon be republished with a fifth. The phrase in the next sentence, meaning a "rendezvous outside the law," is from the first poem in the cycle; *buiten rede en wet* on the following page is "outside reason and law."

the story of how they came to be. "It was magnificent, I wouldn't have missed it for anything." He was standing in the attic, I was on the stairs, one step lower than him. His face no longer had the nervous, fearful expression of someone living in a battle against a fate he can't understand. I felt something like envy. The longing to do this thing—all I lacked was the courage. My situation could have easily taken this Achterbergian turn. I wasn't lacking in courage—this solution would have been a mistake. But now here it's different, and yet still the same *afspraak buiten de wet*. This possibility, of doing the exact opposite of what I believe necessary to do or not do. How many examples of this there are in my own life! And I believe that this choice, to be *buiten rede en wet*, isn't always the worst one. In decisive situations, I have often trusted *that* choice. There is a strange self-affirmation in it. It's not only vanity, as I often trick myself into believing in aggressive/depressive moments. Not vanity. Self-affirmation—experiencing one's own self beyond its boundaries in a way, and then pulling this Beyond back within its boundaries. These are liminal experiences. I really am capable of genuine deep devotion then. When I look at Hanna, I know that I am not only taking. Even though I'm not aware of being the giver. I so often feel ashamed of having received too much, of being worse at giving or relinquishing than the other person. She says the same thing about herself.

When I think about Barbara, or my parents, I feel

like a different person. This feeling fits into the present-day situation in a remarkable way. It provides a contrast with it. Makes me think of responsibility, of having to care for others at an early age. The feeling stays with me and I don't mind when it turns up. It imposes a task on me: to summon up this aspect of life with Hanna as well. Is this what Buber calls the sanctification of an evil impulse? I struggle with all my might against simply playing a game, experiencing moments unconnected with anything else. Am I capable of it? I've been able to keep this from being only a sexual relationship. I wasn't looking for a fling for its own sake. Even in what one might see as a fling. A fling as such has no creative depth, only breadth, an extensive quality. Only an encounter has depth. These two things, a fling and an encounter, are always liable to turn into each other. A fling imposes no obligations. An encounter calls upon the whole person. This is my struggle. I think Hanna sees it the same way I do. I'll ask her. Thinking about her father. Fear of him, almost, and of scandal. But only in passing moments. Even now I'm trying to protect myself. It's despicable, I think so myself—not being in control of this eternal calculation, these neurasthenic impulses.

The times when I write in this diary are my true moments of contemplation. It is a wellspring, my only chance to escape the lies. Yet still so far from the truth of my nature. All the unlived possibilities too, which haven't been able to form my nature. Is longing enough?

For me, it's just a sign that I'm not yet totally a lost cause. I'm often in such uncharted territory, and then feel like a pioneer, far from my homeland. With courage, strength, endurance, venturesomeness, otherwise he wouldn't be a pioneer. And then at night, by the campfire, a feeling of abandonment, homesickness, alienation steals over him. He gets used to it slowly, or never. Someday his children will be locals. I've had more than enough of this feeling already.

The poems I've written lie behind me like something incomprehensible. And the ones before me are no less so. Maybe there won't be any more poems. One always thinks that, = "the last one!"

People are coming into the room, I'll stop writing now. What will night bring.

**Friday, 3/17.** Home again since Wednesday.[21] Four days, a miracle. Had no idea such a thing existed. After the body was liberated, so was the soul. A slow burning, from tenderness to intimacy. Her natural fear, and natural pleasure, when it happened. I understood why men with syphilis think a virgin can cure them. A deep idea. Behind it lies the wish to experience sexuality anew. To start over. For me, too, it was like my past was

21. That is, back with the Rientsmas, on Wallerstraat, after staying with Hanna and the Bakkers on Tak van Poortvlietstraat.

wiped out. What remained of my earlier life came from a different world.

Natural tenderness, consideration. Unforgettably deep understanding. And at the same time, a mirror for myself. "So, that's what I am."

Then, the last afternoon, alone in the little room, an attack of deepest depression, despair. I hope my marriage isn't destroyed. Even though it has irreparable wounds, I'm sure of that. Even a child can't patch it up. And mustn't. What a terrible burden that would be. I think about Gertrud less bitterly and angrily now. We are so alone, alongside each other, against each other. She has never been a mirror for me. Only a radical challenge, shaking me up, a call I followed. I needed to follow it. And even now this call sounds inside me. When Hanna came into the room she stayed with me, surprised and sad, until it was over. The next day she wrote me that even if she now feels some of my despair, she is carrying me in her heart, twice as strong. A simple, straightforward letter.

Conversation with Evert about religious forms and new traditions—went nowhere. I was totally off form and said only incoherent things. He was visibly taken aback, annoyed. Later he said I have no grasp of the topic. Even though the first thing I'd said was "I don't know"! Everything I said after that was just proof that I didn't.

That feeling again, the certainty felt by those who are uncertain: Kafka's pessimism. There is an emperor somewhere, who sits issuing commands—but where, and what do these commands mean for us? Revelation— where is it, where was it ever? Is it unattainable. A mystical sense of some lost earlier oneness. This despair, then, expresses the longing for this connectedness more than any longing could. It is almost like being blinded when the Eternal reveals itself. In the blindness of despair is the luminous closeness of God. That, too, is an experience I had that afternoon.

The next day I read Kierkegaard. Isn't sin often the only way to acknowledge the divine, through our distance from it. My paradoxical ability to experience must be connected to the fact that I do the opposite thing and in this self-avoidance experience the entirely "other." But that's hardly Original Sin. So, then, are tax collectors, criminals, and whores the closest to God? Since the lie of playacting and pretense is the least alive in them? They are so completely earthly and temporal that they attract the lightning bolts of eternity most powerfully. A certain amount of honesty too!

How will things develop between me and Hanna? Will the girl link herself to me so strongly that she gets hurt? If only she could feel everything that's deep inside me and in herself, her halfheartedness might disappear. When Gertrud saw her handwriting,[22] she said: "You

22. Keilson's wife practiced handwriting analysis, and Keilson often praised her "almost incomprehensible second

need to help this girl in a different way, not with counseling. She needs to find a man who loves her very much—who makes her feel everything, deeply. Not halfway, like a game." This spontaneous comment of hers was surely exactly right.

Spent all morning on my letter to Jan.[23] His letter to Gertrud broke the rules of relations between men and women among friends. Letters between husbands and wives, like their dealings in life, are allowed to break those rules, but not letters between friends. I can't say anything to him directly. It took me a week to figure out how to write to him. There is a blunted edge in it that will hurt him, but he'll have to accept it, because I didn't give him an opening to attack what I said. This is the first time I've ever broken with a man like this. Poor devil, Jan. I don't know what else I can say to him.

**Saturday, 3/18.** Letter from Gertrud. Very serious. She has to talk to me. Rudi must have showed her my poems, the ones I wrote for Hanna. Plus there's a misunderstanding and misjudgment of the Jan situa-

---

sight." Keilson retold on many occasions the anecdote that "when she saw Hitler's handwriting for the first time in the early thirties, she said, 'This man is going to engulf the world in flames.' She said it not with hate, but calmly, soberly diagnosing. And he did engulf the world in flames, or tried to" (*Neue Rundschau*, Hans Keilson special issue 120:4 [2009]: 21).

23. Jan Thomassen, who would commit suicide in 1951.

tion. She says I am the reason why Jan opened up to her and revealed the abyss inside him. It's her old dilettantish magical thinking yet again, always looking for a cause outside of the person who does something. It will be a difficult conversation, if she even listens to me at all. Even when she doesn't say anything, that doesn't mean she's listening. It is basically clear to me that a separation has never been as much in the realm of possibility as it is now. Not because of Hanna. Because of our totally different natures.

Here behind my desk I've said everything I have to say to her. That at least gives me the feeling of having said it for once. This is the conflict we've had from the very first day we were together. Unresolved! And it turned me into a writer.

**3/22. Wednesday.**   Home over the weekend with Gertrud and Barbara. In the morning when we were alone in the room, the child stroked my arm and said: Dear Tata. Nice Tata.[24] She looked at me with her big eyes, beaming, deep. At first I didn't pay as much attention to Gertrud as I would have liked to. I wasn't trying to hide anything with my behavior. I have no desire to hide anything. That would be betrayal and hypocrisy. Since I wasn't being forced in any way, I could only

24. A Jewish form of "Daddy." The fact that Keilson was her father was a closely guarded secret.

gradually start to express my feelings for her as she and I both wanted. When she said "But you never say a word to me anymore when we make love" I could have burst into tears. Is it possible, can someone follow two parts of his nature that are so different and not feel one of them as a lie and a betrayal? There's the same "I" behind them both, isn't there. Splitting? Fugue state? It was Gide, wasn't it, who rebelled against restrictions forcibly imposed on human nature? With Hanna I am often just as distant and estranged—but still, a marriage is different. I feel very powerfully what it means to have a family. My problems with Gertrud are still there without Hanna. I don't let her in. That's another story. I often feel like everything sinks so deeply into me—the conflict that is not a conflict between objects but rather the process in a person, a subject. When I raise it up into the light of day, it becomes horrible. I'm so distant and removed from everything. Supported by Gertrud's confidence and trust. Does she realize I'm trying to enlarge my inner possibilities before the end of the war gives me outward possibilities too? Am only slowly resigning myself to the fact that the moral concepts I used to apply can't be turned into a universal principle. It's not permanent—I know that. But an experience not fully undergone can often be so oppressive and difficult.

My child is mine. The bond that so often disappears between a man and a woman is forming between the child and me. First, Gertrud has to get better. I owe her this time to rest and recuperate. And how will Hanna emerge from all this? Her strength is growing. I can feel it.— When I was sitting with Olga G.,[25] I understood her better than ever. My listening in silence was more mature, and it will accomplish more than before. I noticed that in the letter she wrote me, which I was so happy to get. It might seem from the outside that I am adrift, but inwardly I am truer than ever before.

**Friday. 3/24**

Again a sense of disaster haunting me. Is this the perception of an objective mind or the psychological fallout from a conflict of conscience? It's like when you take another path to the goal than the one you'd originally planned, but, having chosen it, never give it up to the bitter end, so as to appreciate the strange new beauty of the surrounding landscape. God gives this sign too. I am fighting like a giant to clear this path in the wilderness. When I wrest a poem out of it, it gives me this feeling that I am paying back a debt.

Jo and Fiet's wedding in Utrecht.[26] Very clear view of them both as they stood under the chuppah. Am I so

25. Olga Gülcher, for whom Gertrud worked for a time as a housekeeper after Keilson went underground, or perhaps her daughter, also named Olga.

26. Joop Andriesse and Sofie Hes, also in hiding at the Rientsmas' for a short time. The chuppah, mentioned in the next sentence, is the canopy under which the couple stand in the main

far removed from it now that I can no longer reach this pure simplicity? Orthodoxy, thy name is: Simplicity. The service didn't fail to move me. Then in de Haas's house, the modest meal. The whole time, Jo looked at Fiet with his small, almond-shaped eyes—searchingly, sad, loving. As though purely and completely worried about her. How strong and manly his love seemed. Since I was imagining myself in his place, I felt it very strongly inside of me. I saw Gertrud and later Hanna step under the chuppah. But Gertrud stood there like the beat of my heart, like a cry to God. Hanna: sad, alone, fragile, the way I love her. Her face is changing so much. Her being.

Talked to her today. She asked me how I can have both her and Gertrud inside me. The question didn't come as a surprise. She asked it very calmly and deliberately, as though she had asked it a thousand times. Our closeness when we talk to each other, so calm and trusting, has a rare, liberating delicacy and intimacy. I am very grateful to her for it. No bitter word from her mouth. Tact, restraint. But Gertrud stood like a cry to God, inside me too. Finally, finally. Why have you kept that from me. Now I am yours. I stayed quiet and calm. What will happen now. I no longer ask myself what I have to do, I just do it.

---

symbolic act of a Jewish wedding, comparable to the exchange of rings in the Christian ceremony.

Evening. After the walk. She was so quiet when I told her about my life in Berlin. She absolutely froze. I could feel it. We stood there and I saw her face in the dim light. It had a different expression than usual. A consuming fire from within. The whole blaze transformed into great inner strength. This love is at the same time suffering. Duse[27] must have loved and suffered like this.

Feeling that becomes entirely internal. "I can't bear both," she said, "both you and the life you're telling me about." Almost as soon as she said these words. I saw in her walk, felt in the swaying of her body, how she was changing. Love, love, nothing but love. Deep understanding. Affinity. I was again as close to her as we were at the beginning, when I saw her inner face. It's strange how her suffering exhilarates me. I came to her rescue, started talking about something else, but my soul had grown light and inspired, winged. While she suffered. And at the same time I understood her, felt with her. Thoughts raced through my mind: Was I doing the right thing? Who can say? Then we danced with each other. Incredible tension that our bodies couldn't ease. How I love her, would do anything for her. "I'm scared

27. Legendary Italian actress Eleanora Duse (1858–1924), famous for emotionally inhabiting her characters rather than using gestures and expressions of conventional theatricality, and for her passionate love affairs with poet Gabriele d'Annunzio and others.

of you," she said. "You are so strong." But I'm not the one in control. The stakes are often higher for me—more dangerous.

**Tuesday 3/28/44**
Went to see Dr. Fetter in The Hague yesterday.[28] He's been sick for a long time, I haven't talked to him since before Christmas. He had said he would circulate ten of my poems. As I sat in his waiting room in the church on the Laan with its wonderful name,[29] he would come out of his consultation room to tell each new visitor to come in. He looked tired and pale. Not like a bearer of God's word—like someone exhausted from bearing a burden, bearing it too long.

Eventually it was my turn. We sat across from each other next to the little gas stove. He asked me for Gertrud's address so he could send her 25 fl. Then he asked me why I didn't go to an organization for help. The question confused me. Because D.Div. Klein[30] had asked me exactly the same thing last time and seemed

28. J.C.A. Fetter (1885–1959), involved with the Remonstrant parish in The Hague from 1933 to 1949. He had studied literature (with a thesis on Ibsen) and psychoanalysis.

29. The Church of the Remonstrant Brotherhood, on Laan 22. Jews in hiding were given shelter in the building during the Occupation.

30. François Kleijn (1887–1970), who tried unsuccessfully to set up an official church asylum for Jews.

almost insulted that I was taking care of things myself. Fetter was nervous, his eye was visibly twitching. I explained that I thought it was better if I did it myself. Unlike last time, when it seemed that this exact line of reasoning was what won him over, he was apparently no longer susceptible to it. "Why don't you let Henny de Jong[31] and me organize something for you" etc. Then I told him, since he asked, about Gertrud and about our relationship—that we weren't officially married. He listened to everything quietly, didn't answer in any pointed or definite way but also showed no signs of friendliness or agreeing with me. Then I asked him whether he'd read the poem[32] and what he thought of it. "Nothing," he said. Then, more firmly: "Yes, well, it won't mean anything to the reader." I was not taken aback in the least, I can easily imagine people to whom this poem would have nothing to say. "It didn't to me either," he went on. "It means nothing to me. I was dumbfounded. I don't understand it, I do not understand how someone can be a Jew, as you say, as you truthfully say you are, and write a poem like that. I can't understand it." I don't remember what I said next, but it certainly wasn't meant either to calm him down or to

31. Another pastor; possibly, judging from a letter Keilson wrote to Gertrud at the time, the one who tried to look after Keilson's parents, in Delft and in Westerbork transit camp.
32. Keilson had published the poem "In Memoriam" under the pseudonym Alexander Kailand in March 1940.

excite him. So what happened next was the result of [*illegible*], where I just happened to play the role of the catalyst.

"You're the third one today, always these Jews, don't take it the wrong way but always these problems with the Jews!" And he threw his books onto the floor with a loud bang. Here we were, in Dr. Fetter's own consultation room, and I realized that I was treating him. I stayed sympathetically impassive. I looked at this gray, tired, older man, who had doubted deeply and probably never overcome his doubt, and his face reminded me of a boy who's had his toys taken away. "Always these Jews," he repeated, "they rejected Christ, they excommunicated Spinoza—over and over, again and again, they've provoked extraordinary responses from other peoples. Why are our boys in the camps, in prisons, why is Dr. Van Veen in custody because his daughter had Jews in the house? Enough already, this has got to stop!"

He was beside himself. Never in my life have I heard someone who wasn't an anti-Semite talk like that. So completely in line with the anti-Semitic terminology. I remembered what Leen[33] had told me about Fetter: how his initial reaction to National Socialism had been positive (obviously—he was a student of Jung's!), and

33. Leendert Swaneveld, described in the entry of October 19, p. 79.

34

how later he'd spoken publicly about his disenchantment with them over their solution to the Jewish question. So here he was in front of me, like someone bemoaning the disappointment he'd suffered, because it had destroyed his ideals, ideals he was loath to give up. "You're a nice fellow," he told me, "you mustn't take what I'm saying personally. But the Jews are always smart, clever, slippery. So I'm called out to Paviljoensgracht because some Jews in hiding have 3,000 fl. to give me for safekeeping. I go, even though it's basically none of my business. Or this morning, someone comes to see me because he wants a life insurance policy and I have to declare that he's been baptized. But he isn't baptized. And now here you are. I have to tell you, you're a pleasant fellow, but you're also pedantic. You come in here, say it's a good poem, ask me what people think of it." He could have gone on and on like that for a long time. "Then you ask me whether I've heard of your wife as a graphologist. I haven't, and you've made me feel stupid."

"Yes," I said, very calm and composed, because I could see that Fetter was suffering from things he didn't have the power to change, even if he wanted to, "maybe those are Jewish traits. You're right, there are a lot of things about us that other people must find hard to take."

"Oh, you know, when you run across a Dutchman abroad they make a very unpleasant impression too—badly behaved, loud, horrible. But so do the Jews. I can understand why someone would marry a Jewess, but the whole family that comes crowding round with her? Unbearable."

"You must find me unbearable too, going around door-to-door with my poem like someone selling bad soap. To you it seems pushy. But you're not looking at the other side. You forget, I've worked as a psychologist, I've sat in my consultation room and had people come to see me just like they come to see you. When someone decides to take that step, the step I took, there must be a great need behind it, pushing him to do it."

"Yes, of course, but an incomprehensible poem like that . . . And I don't understand how you can be a Jew and marry a non-Jewish woman. There are the Orthodox Jews who follow the laws, I can't understand them at all. Carrying your handkerchief with two knots tied in it on Saturdays but not in your pocket, what kind of religious issue is that? Then there are the fully assimilated ones, who don't bother with any of it. They're even worse. And now here you are, a third type, I can figure you out even less." He was completely at sea. But I was glad I was talking like this to someone who could have been my father, and glad that he could find some peace with me.

Gradually the situation he was in began to dawn on him. "It's too much, it's too much! Jews all the time, we can't take it anymore." All the while I was thinking about my poem about Jews. We Jews![34] One often can't take it anymore. Fetter was being honest, this was what he thought. He wasn't trying to hide behind the Bible.

Maybe you know about what they're building in Palestine, what's going on there. But they're locking horns there too. But maybe it's possible to find a new tradition after all? Not the old one, with its laws that have become meaningless, magical activities without spiritual content. Do you think that's possible? Yes, I hope so. I'm amazed to realize how much I increasingly long for traditional religious forms. "I see . . . Is that Buber's path as well?" As far as I understand it, yes. He too supports a movement of religious renewal. "Doesn't he have an Aryan wife too?" He does. The conversation grew more personal. I told him that I often went to see Jews and helped them get through the problems that erupted due to their long periods in hiding. Typical Jewish qualities. As a result of my open admissions, my not trying to whitewash the Jews, Fetter slowly came back to his senses. His eyelid stopped twitching. A beautiful, deep, kind

34. "We Jews," published with other poems on the same theme by "A Jewish Poet: Alexander Kailand" in March 1938. The poem begins (in prose paraphrase): "We Jews are, in this world, a dirty pile of cheap money, devalued by God. He doesn't take us out of circulation; he throws us away, calls us back—we pay all debts. So we wander from hand to hand, our hunchback bent, never rubbed clean."

look came into his eyes. He had made it through the crisis.

"I have to tell you, personally I think your poem is not bad, not bad at all. There are a few difficult lines in it. But how can a Jew write about Christ like that?" I told him about the book that Dr. Hellma had showed me, about the Jesus question in modern Judaism.[35] He didn't know it. "Still," he said—

May I speak honestly, Domine? "Of course." There's something that I don't understand. I've heard that you've studied Jung, so how is it that you don't use the concept of the collective unconscious to explain the Jewish character, Jewish fate and Jewish life? His ears pricked up. "You're right," he said. "I don't understand that either, actually." And then, I went on, I know that you spoke in public about National Socialism, after you had tried to judge it positively and objectively at first, but later you spoke just as publicly about how disappointed you were in the Nazis, with their solution to the Jewish question. He sat up straight and looked at me. "Where did you hear that?" I must know you better than you know me, Doctor. "No one knows that, not one member of my parish knows I said that. And now here you are, and you

35. Possibly Albert Helman (1903–96), the editor of *De Gemeenschap* from 1925 to 1931 who had been working to help Jewish refugees since his return from Mexico in 1939. The book was likely Gösta Lindeskog's *The Question of Jesus in Modern Judaism* (1938).

know it. It's true. I thought 50% of what the Nazis were was good." A dangerously high number, I put in. "I eventually realized that myself. It was a great letdown for me. Personally, I think your poem . . . Don't you want to change the lines that are unclear?"

"'With my misery . . .'" I said.[36]

"Yes, that one for instance."

"It means . . ." I gave him my usual explanation, the one I've already told several people. "It is καιρός,"[37] I said. "The misery of the Jews is the καιρός for the non-Jews."

"Oh, that's how you see it? I didn't know that. Now I understand better. It's only Christ you can't accept."

"Not as a mediator. It is a danger for God, as Rilke said." Fetter said nothing, nodded. "And that he saved one part of mankind and not the other—that is unacceptable. And the direct relationship with God is lost."

"Now I understand better. You mustn't think I'm an

36. From "In Memoriam," a poem addressed to "Jesus, my friends' friend and Lord." (Line 1: "You human being, before whom I cannot bow.") The line is "With my misery gauge its meaning," i.e., "ascertain my misery's meaning," or perhaps "With my misery measure your people's meaning"—it is a difficult line.

37. *Kairos*, an ancient Greek word meaning the right moment, the opportune time—time measured not by chronology but by purpose or meaning. In Christianity, it refers to "the fullness of time" when God acts.

anti-Semite. I wouldn't talk like this to a Nazi." Doctor, I do understand you, truly. "I've always been in good health, but this winter I've had eye problems—iritis." It's too much, Doctor, I know, it really is too much, I know. It is an honor for me that you've been able to find a little peace with me here, relax a bit. Truly, an honor for me. He laughed softly. "I'll give you the 25 fl. now, that way I won't have to send it to your wife." He gave it to me.

"I understand you better," he said. I stood up.

"Do you know, the thing about your poem—people don't have the peace and quiet it takes to read it slowly and attentively." I know, I said. I had hoped that you would take the time to read it attentively. The attention is all that matters to me. Nothing else. "Come back and see me again, I'd be happy to speak with you further." He walked me to the door. "And you mustn't think that—because I said those things at the beginning—we all get tired sometimes . . ." You don't need to apologize, Doctor. I believe I do understand your situation, really. "Goodbye, come again."—

**Tuesday.** Saw Gertrud in Amsterdam. She looked radiant. Her hat and coat, slim face, spruced up a bit the way I like. Thinner. Her diet is working. She feels better. In good spirits. A magnificent afternoon with her. "You write me such cold, businesslike letters." I was shocked. What, I thought, I have that little self-control?

And I felt so affectionate toward her.— Kissed her warmly. Before leaving the train station.

Evening, saw Hanna briefly. It was the day Ev and Fiet were leaving. She barely shook my hand and didn't dare look at me. So timid, yearning. Even after spending Sunday night here with me again. Intimate, loving, natural. But it's definitely me who takes the lead. She must feel so alone with the people she's staying with, watching as Ev and Fiet left, full of energy, in love, for freedom and danger.— I felt a pang. What have I done, I thought. But it would have been even harder for her if things were different.

In the entry about Fetter I forgot to describe the little things. Why I had a non-Jewish wife. The children were non-Jewish. "Ruth," I said.[38] He nodded. Besides, a person's love life is an individual question for everyone. People have to decide for themselves.

**Wednesday, 29th.**   I've just been reading in Fetter's *Nieuwe Kracht uit het oude Woord*.[39] And understood for the first time Abraham's sacrifice. It suddenly dawned on me as something I was familiar with—I made this sacrifice when I stepped back from writing my poems.

38. The biblical convert to Judaism and model of kindness.
39. *New Strength from the Old Word* (1940). The following sentence is in Dutch, not German; apparently writing the Dutch title switched Keilson into Dutch temporarily.

A creative surge followed. You live for years with something you know, live your life with it, and then one day see it anew and recognize it with a shock.

**Friday, 31st.**   Saw a very old married couple yesterday. He was hobbling along with two canes, she was blind. He limped laboriously down the street while she carefully held on tight to him. He was her support. They got onto the tram. When they got off again, I saw how they talked to each other. He was apparently telling her where they were: On a traffic island near the Holland Rail station in The Hague. He carefully turned himself around in a little circle until he was facing the direction they needed to go in to cross the tracks. She had her hand on his shoulder, gentle, soft, you could feel how it almost floated above him. Because she couldn't see him he was still her hero, leading her safely, hobbling along on two canes. How did they do their shopping? Or maybe they lived in an old-age home. A happy old age, maybe there was still love between them. She couldn't see how fragile he was and maybe felt like more of an invalid than him. He could still be her protector, her knight in shining armor. Maybe he had to live this long and grow this old to make this dream of his early years a reality. Before, when she could see, it hadn't come true, but now . . . I couldn't think of any other explanation for their harmony and contentment.

Yesterday Hanna said: "For you this is only something that's happened, a beautiful experience. But for me . . ." Then silence. I understood her. She was sad, because she had discovered something, had had a life experience, that left her feeling sad and alone. I wrote her a long letter that night, she was happy to get it today. "You can say it better, truer, more beautifully, than I can myself." Really? I asked. "It's just how you described it." I had written about the transformation she was going through.

An embarrassing situation the next day, neither of us found it especially pleasant but it was resolved thanks to her natural perceptiveness. She understands more when you talk to her. With her I am wiping out my whole past—all the mistakes, all that ignorance, I can truly get rid of them now. It's very liberating.

On Sunday, very calmly, she asked me how I take this situation and harmonize it inside me with Gertrud. I answered, just as calmly, that I've wanted very badly to be with someone young. Not because Gertrud was too old—no. But it was easier for me to understand a woman than a girl. Now it was like I was making up for what I hadn't had before and hadn't been capable of. It had stayed inside me like a blind spot. And she had entirely filled it in. This is true, in a way I am rarely capable of being. For example, I often think about how I can't write her any more letters that might compromise me with her father later. I was horrified by this thought of covering my back. I fought it for a long time. But now

I've written it down after all. I can't let it get the upper hand.

Stefan George's translations are wonderful.[40] Especially his Rossetti, his Swinburne. Even if George had never written anything else, these would make him a great poet.

But what a poet Rossetti was first! I try in vain to achieve this crystalline transparency and Bach-like music in my poems. I suddenly understand him better. Verlaine in French, too. *Avant de toute chose la musique!*[41] His best poems are almost . . . Chinese. I know no higher praise.

I approach art musically. I hear from the sentence how the melody should continue. I look for the right continuation but often can't find it. So little success. A lot that seems usable at first has to be thrown out later.

My need to express myself has become a necessity like never before. I do almost nothing else anymore. Except play the violin. There, too, I find the possibility of a fulfilling dialogue. Mozart. Yesterday, at a movie about Mozart set in Salzburg, I had a vision of the bomb-

40. Stefan George (1868–1933), major German poet. His 1929 book of translations includes works by the English Dante Gabriel Rossetti, Algernon Charles Swinburne, and Ernest Dowson; the Danish writer Jens P. Jacobsen; Dutch poets Willem Kloos and Albert Verwey; and the Belgian poet Emile Verhaeren.

41. "Music above all else!" Paul Verlaine's 1874 poem "Art poétique" opens *"De la musique avant toute chose."*

ing of Salzburg. Leaning against Mozart's grave was a grieving angel. Salzburg, Mozart, Mozart, bombing!—Not that rhyme!—This was the constant scream inside me. Then, as Beethoven's music played, I saw the statue of a girl's body appear on-screen. The chastity of the image, the meekness—what I had felt myself—gripped me so powerfully that I stayed in my seat to watch the movie a second time. And I had the same feeling again. A world rose up before me. Greed was gone, natural joy and beauty had broken through. I was in a state of rapture!

**Saturday. 4/1.** Days when I can find my composure only in writing poems. Intense concentration—work! Recopy, scrutinize, shift things around. Endlessly. After initial satisfaction comes deepest despair. Will it ever turn out as something good?

**Wednesday 4/19.**   Haven't written for a long time. Feelings of indecision, but not between one woman and the other. Instead, between me—solitude, my own rhythm—and adapting to another person at all. It's almost over with Gertrud. She feels a firmer determination in me and it's true, I feel that, deep down. If Barbara weren't so sweet, always pitter-pattering between us. Gertrud and I are close to the breaking point. Her primitive aggressiveness and excitability will drive us apart. But I can't make problems now. Her intense conflict about going back to Germany . . .

Later, here—Hanna. Her naturalness, sadly a little corrupted now. She cries a lot. How wonderful she is. A string vibrates, resonates deep inside me, when I'm with her. Plus I know that this isn't the last song that's going to be played on it. Is it only an existential experience? As a truth, or true as an untruth? I feel so deeply that my boundaries are being pulled at, that I'm expanding.

Started a prose piece.[42] What a relief to write about

42. The events that Keilson would turn into *Comedy in a Minor Key* took place between April 14 and 18. The Dutch couple

people, lives, dialogue, events, instead of purely personal experiences and conditions of the soul. I learned a lot from Katherine Mansfield.[43] But have not achieved her concentration, her delicate floating in solid three-dimensional space. Have to keep working.

A graphologist said: This is a man who will suddenly disappear, and turn up again ten years later!— Saw German secret police in the train. One of them was definitely epileptic. German propaganda from epileptics!— I saw how he was looking around.

So immersed in writing that I hardly understand science anymore.

### Tuesday [actually Monday], 4/24

Three German officers in charge of the inundation of Rotterdam.[44] In private life: a tailor, a dentist, and a bookkeeper. And also idiots!

The Dutch grocer in charge of the underground in the district! One man!

---

in the book, Wim and Marie, are partially based on Hanna's hosts, Arie and Evy Bakker, while Keilson said late in life that he identified with the Jewish character in hiding, Nico. See Introduction.

43. English short-story writer from New Zealand (1888–1923), whom Hanna was translating at the time.

44. By early 1944, the Germans had made plans to partially flood the country, artificially raising the groundwater near Rotterdam, to impede the Allied advance. They did so that summer.

Slowly, slowly, crystallizing inside me again. It has to do with the story I'm writing. Really it's a question of character. I often feel so cut off from my own life.

Deepest bond with Gertrud. Stirring the depths that attract and repel. Primal things! Primal instincts! My indecisive formlessness (seen from within)—it's productive. Work, work.

Asked Razum,[45] who is hiring new actors for the German Theater in the Netherlands, how long he thinks this all will last.

"Forever!"

"Very true" was my answer: "Very true, you don't know how true that is."

**6/18.** After a long time I feel the need for this journal again. The rush of writing is behind me. The novella is finished. And a poem. My own life, conscience, claim my attention and energy again.

The fiction writing surprised me again and again; I think I've made several discoveries about the possibilities of prose. Talked to Gertrud about it, and suddenly out

---

45. Keilson ran into Hannes Razum (1907–94), whom he knew in Germany, in The Hague. This "unusual reunion" and their conversation forms one of the great scenes in his memoir (*My House*, ch. 21): "What had I expected from our meeting? What had he? Two men had sat there and tried to step outside of their time, for thirty, maybe forty-five minutes, by concealing much of what had to do with their lives in that time."

came her incredible deep maturity, understanding, empathy, sharing. I need that as urgently as H's loving affection and devotion. And yet—I'm so split. I lead my vigorous life in two directions. Almost unconflicted! For as long as I stayed productive. I think morality was the invention of an unproductive person. For that reason alone it is not of divine origin! God himself is obviously productive.—

How Gertrud is changing in the significance I give her. Is she really as attached to me, dependent on me, as she says? Or is that just her unconscious compensation? I understand what marriage is—a form of human companionship—better now that I am transcending it. I so want to raise our child with her, i.e. see how Barbara herself will grow and change. Gertrud told me her dream where Barbara finished the song that Gertrud couldn't sing to the end.

And yet, who knows if I can do it. Whether my productivity doesn't depend on living out a perpetual split. Whether the artist—I write the word with a shudder—won't die off with the return to the family. What I accuse Gertrud of actually applies to me of course. Maybe I wasn't cut out to be both. It's too bad Groenevelt isn't enough of an artist.[46] He could have given me advice.

What a wonderful thing a girl is, and I'm already

46. Dutch psychiatrist A. Groeneveld, active since the late 1920s in the first Amsterdam Medisch Opvoedkundig Bureau (a

afraid I'm mistreating her. I often feel a longing for her virgin state—[*illegible*]—when she looked in the mirror. Again and again deep connection, attunement, when we're together. Her restraint, her passivity, gives my fantasies enough room, enough freedom, to be turned into action. If we stayed together forever—would it still be like that? I sometimes think about looming disasters— Then try to banish these thoughts by reminding myself of the neurasthenic aspect in them. But who knows?

It's the juxtaposition of the two women, stronger and sharper in me than ever. But more elaborated. What in Gerd Klaaß[47] is and remains fuzzy and vain I am trying to bring to consciousness, a sorrowful awareness of my artistic path. I have to get through it and come out the other side. I struggle not to make Gertrud the victim of my moods, since she is at such a disadvantage in many ways. I don't know if I can manage that. So far I have. I'm not pulling the wool over anyone's eyes. I often

---

psychiatric-educational clinic for children). Keilson would work there after 1945.

47. Gerd Klaaß, the German emigrant with whom Keilson and Gertrud lived first in Amsterdam, then in Naarden, at Van Hall-laan 15. His wife, Traudelise Katz, was the niece of Mrs. Adelaar-Fürth, whose sister had introduced Keilson and Gertrud in Berlin and who had arranged for his residence permit in the Netherlands. Klaaß and Keilson published anthologies of poetry under the joint pseudonym Benjamin Cooper.

feel like I need to talk to her about it, because I know that no one would understand what I'm feeling better than Gertrud herself. She has it in her to understand it, definitely. But not now—she doesn't have the strength for it now, and of course the current circumstances. It would be brutally heartless, to her and to our child, if I came to her with my problems now.

6/21.   Lieske[48] saying good morning to her pets when she fed them: Hello, Boy! Here you go, Chys! Oh, you can hardly wait, can you, Goes!

It was dark in the veterinarian's waiting room. No windows. A man was sitting there, and I couldn't see if he had an animal with him or not. Finally the doctor opened the glass door and I saw that the man was carrying a bunny in a bag.— "Who will open the door for you when you come home?" the little boy asked.— "Is the world round, Daddy, is it, is it? Then I want to live at the end of the world." "Why?" "Because then I can look out over the whole world."

The cleaning woman says: "No, I wasn't there, no I wasn't *almost* there either. And then there was a movie night in Old Scheveningen, and I wasn't *almost* there either."

48. Lies, the elder daughter of the Rientsmas; the animals were guinea pigs.

The newspaper boy in Rotterdam pushing his cart over the platform, shouting: "I used to be in the market square selling bananas!" Pitch of his voice: - - - - - - - - _ _.

Hanna writes that she has to force herself to feel things she doesn't feel. That she feels unsure and indecisive with me. She is very honest, even where she isn't entirely.

Things aren't how they used to be in the core of our relationship. Other things are coming into the foreground too much. I don't know what's going on inside her. I imagine she's at a loss herself, about me too. I'm ultimately the cause of it, of course. Her feeling that it's "hopeless" between us is right. In the end, she'll be left all alone. I'm taking advantage of her. Powerful conflict between my temperament and my attraction to a young woman. If only I were more in harmony with myself! Every time we're close it makes her feel the gap that ultimately lies between us.

I often want to stop, since I have the feeling it's all run dry.

I am not as honest with her as I used to be—I'm forcing myself too, I can imagine that what she feels is just the mirror image of my own state. Every now and then I more consciously remember what she was for me before: the most wonderful mirror for me. If only she'd stayed that! I still love her delicacy and warmth. Tomorrow I'll talk to her.

## Saturday. 7/15

No doubt about it, I'm in an extremely miserable state. Reality isn't enough for me anymore. Its charms are too weak to pull me out of my depression. So I look for new stimulation. Sometimes it's work. Sometimes it's women. Like the night when I went to a fat m . . . But I was impotent. It didn't work. I was glad, and grateful, when I saw that I still had a core inside me, still intact.

Are my poems too much outgrowths of my will, of artistic labor, rather than creativity? I feel such aversion to them afterward. But whenever I see Gertrud and the child, something is touched in me, not only affection or love but a huge body of water suddenly swelling and spilling up onto the shore.

My feelings for Hanna have changed very much. All the tremendous happiness has given way to a deep life experience, partly strange and paralyzing, partly heavy (in terms of weight). Her sadness, her childlike openness, touch me. That's the good side of our friendship. What's harder for me to face is a feeling I wouldn't have thought I had so much of: sadism. Liking to torture her, make her suffer. And then when I see her, it hurts me at the same time, so much that I could cry. On top of that, I'm so suggestible with other people. I live off them like a vampire. But then don't use what they try to give me. I haven't entirely lost the H.K. from before. Celibate bachelors often don't make the best husbands, Gide says. That's the case with me, to some extent.

My double nature exhausts me. But the more doubled and split one is, the more one's an artist. That's the unity I'm striving for. And I often think about the Jews in the camps. A trip with illegal documents. I'm drawn to death. More and more. Attached to it like a fly on flypaper—first one leg, eventually all six. I don't play music anymore, I can't. First it was a sore finger. Then rage and aversion to it.

I don't believe my own feelings anymore. It's all an act, a put-on! Only the gloom and depression is real. I would need to live alone, far from everyone, except only Gertrud and the child sometimes, to slowly pull myself together. I move around too much, I'm too restless.

On my last visit to Amsterdam I heard a story from Inspector W. at Ruth's that I will definitely use for a novel.[49] The situation resolved thanks to the shoe! Two operations.

Talked with Madeleine and Mensingt. Poor guy. I

49. Ruth Simon. Madeleine and Mensingt, mentioned just below, are perhaps the Jewish couple from Cottbus, Germany, in hiding with Ruth and Wolfgang Simon (see *My House*, ch. 18). Inspector W. is surely the Amsterdam police inspector J. Wijnberg, who helped make sure Keilson's fake ID was safe to use. He lived in the same building as the Simons and testified in September 1945 that Hans Keilson had helped falsify passports illegally during the German occupation.

figured that out right away. And she is very sensitive. She could be my angel. I understand something about her life, her eyes tell me. Will I ever see her again?

Two Amsterdam women, cursing at each other. One shouts: "I was arrested for my radio, I don't care who knows it, I etc. But I never ratted on anyone." The other woman—short, gray, glasses, the rat—defended herself: "It was only for ten days." She had taken her husband's arm. A strange picture: the informer couple. New idea of marital solidarity through the act of betrayal. The fight continued on the street.

Bought Thomas Mann, *Jacob* and *Joseph*.[50] Like a reunion. I was so happy to hold them in my hand again. The writing is so magnificent.

Malraux, *The Human Condition*, is almost unbearable.

Talked to Rudi. He asked me if the poems were for Gertrud. I said no. Said that a mix of truth and fiction went into them.[51] He hastily agreed.

Started a Judas poem. Self-portrait. Stuck for now. Maybe it'll turn out.

Does my being lost have a purpose, or is it pointless? Which means: Is it impossible to give it a positive

50. Volumes 1 and 2 of Thomas Mann's tetralogy *Joseph and His Brothers*.

51. Keilson writes "a mix of *Dichtung* and *Wahrheit*," a reference to Goethe's autobiography, *Dichtung und Wahrheit*, whose title is often translated *Poetry and Truth* but is more like *Art and Truth* or *Fiction and Reality*.

purpose? For the *poète maudit*, the causality of getting lost is [*illegible*]. It happens once or twice, but not as cause or effect, merely as life. What lies beyond the calculable is revealed to have causal connections only to the later observer through hindsight.

Slept. In a better mood. Well rested, or because the reality of the sleeping state alleviates the contradictions of the waking state. Sleep suits them better.

**Tuesday 9/6/44**[52]

They say the English are in Rotterdam. They'll reach Delft by tomorrow. Then I'll be free, and can go home. When they march in, part of my life will end too, one that started 20 years ago. This past year will also end, the most critical year in my life. All the powers I have in me were put into action and pulled me in all directions. Under this intense pressure, I wrote poems and fiction. It looks as though I can be productive only with this extreme strain and burden on my conscience and my

52. September 6 was a Wednesday; September 5 came to be known in Dutch history as *Dolle Dinsdag* (Mad Tuesday). Since D-day—the Allied landing in Normandy on June 6, 1944—the tide of the war had turned and the Allies were advancing through western Europe; Antwerp was liberated on September 4. On September 5, reports of an advance through Belgium awakened hopes that Rotterdam and Amsterdam were about to be liberated, as Keilson writes. The Dutch celebrated but their hopes were premature. The first Allied troops would not enter the Netherlands until September 9, and the failure with heavy losses of Operation Market Garden, later in September, ended any chance that the Allies might end the war by Christmas.

other mental apparatuses. In parallel, the wish to protect Gertrud, for her own sake and the sake of the child, who now will soon be my child publicly too. I'm sorry about every harsh word I've written here about Gertrud. It expressed how conflicted I was. I will break up with Hanna. Even though I forgot about her sometimes, I kept going back to her, as though to a melody I liked hearing and sang myself. She, for her part, is feeling the double impact of the war ending and the relationship ending. She wrote me a letter expressing this terrible clash between hope for release and fear of loss. But even in this struggle she is sweet, more gentle and loving than I can say—the very things that made me feel so connected to her.

My poems, too, have almost come to an end. I feel like I've sucked the blood from Hanna the person and from life itself, like a vampire, and used it to feed my poems. The amoral instinct of the poet! The asocial man as exemplary! And meanwhile, seeing Gertrud, which always had such a big effect on me. Our life together is this series of blows. And that's good. It keeps us from getting rigid. But now, when I go home—! For the time being, I still live in fear that something might happen to Gertrud and the child. I want to go home, but I'm still worried about roundups[53] in the trains. Often, very often,

53. The first mention in the diary of razzias: the Nazi roundups carried out in many occupied countries. They would cordon off streets and go door-to-door throughout whole neighborhoods,

I feel intense longing for Gertrud. I will be such a different person. What will become of us. Will we stay here in Holland? Will I be a doctor? Everything still looks very difficult. I am already giving up. Is it just exhaustion from what we've been through, or something more?

But the amount of conscious self-control I've had to muster with Hanna was enormous. I had to rein myself in so much. While she reined me in just by saying "No, please not that!" So simple. Everything was so natural, because everything was welcome to her—even her resistance. Women raise us, teach us, I've never experienced that to such a degree. *Never*. The emancipated woman has lost this whole side of things!

And I'm playing a lot of music again! The first time they've gone together: music and poetry. Goodbye to Mrs. van der Lek, the pianist.[54]

**Thursday**
All the reports turned out to be premature. The English and Americans have crossed the Dutch border, according

---

looking either for Jews and other undesirables, or for men who had not reported for labor service, who would then be shipped off to work in Germany, sometimes in forced-labor camps. Keilson, with his fake ID, was in danger not as a Jew but as a working-age male.

54. Cora van der Lek-Temme, a neighbor. Keilson used to go through the emergency escape route and come down from her attic to play music with her. What kind of "goodbye" this was is not known.

to official reports, but no one knows anything else. The excitement reached its anticlimax. We still have to wait.

Jan B. saved from death, it was practically a miracle! In his papers it said "Shoot him."

There is no poet I have a harder time taking a position on than Rilke. I think about his poetic persona all the time. Reading him more intensively now, I feel an unresolved flood of pros and cons—maybe typical of my own attitude, maybe also characteristic of Rilke's poetry. It can't be reduced to a formula. All the countless literary labels you can use to assign a poet a certain rank or position come up short with him. Is he a closet Romantic? A Baroque poet, a Symbolist, a Decadent? It all becomes so irrelevant once you engage with the man and his work.

The best label is one I heard from Gertrud recently. But it expresses less of a purely literary or poetic quality than a sociological one. Minnesinger.[55] Rilke as the prototypical modern Minnesinger, gushing from one invitation to the next, offering his deep courtly bows— his letters—his poems—to beautiful women, awakening love while not partaking of it—truly, a Minnesinger.

55. The Minnesingers were twelfth-to-fourteenth-century German lyric poets, strongly influenced by the troubadours, whose main theme was *Minne*, or love.

The first impression his poems made on me was of incredible, monstrous weakness—crystallized, purified, and converted into something else. I could almost smell the sweat from the effort. The last time I picked up his poems—because I protect myself, I don't read them very much, the same way he is careful not to read too much poetry by other poets so as not to lose his own music— I was surprised to see how finely wrought they actually are. I had forgotten, or hadn't noticed it before. There's a lot that's magnificent, stunning. But still: this great weakness. A vital weakness. It is all too obvious that he would abandon his wife and child. How much his wife must have suffered from his weakness. Rilke is not a man. It's an open question for me whether he "was" even human. He knew that he "was" not yet a human being, and his efforts were directed at "becoming" one. This was his "being." He was trying to create himself out of the circumstances that a human being is faced with: God, surroundings, tree, landscape, animals. This "turning inward" of surrounding circumstances fed into his love for Russia.[56] For him, the path to humanity detoured

56. The term Keilson puts in quotes is *Inne Werden*, which normally means "realizing" or "becoming aware of," but which for Rilke carries the weight of "internalizing" or "becoming inward": the poet bringing the things of the world deeply into himself, where they ripen and grow.

through the poet. It was a difficult path for him. And it shows his weaknesses, or rather, his formlessness.

You can praise him or criticize him, or both, but the fact remains that he represents a very special case of poet. Not someone who does without so that he can devote himself to being creative, but someone who creates in order to become human. Various biographical facts show this—the way he later became more social, more considerate. He didn't really understand music, knew nothing about the state of things *ante rem*.[57] Or humor. Someone like Stefan George, for all his repellent human qualities, is still human. Whereas Rilke is blank white paper.

Someone like Rossetti is superior to him too. Rossetti seems to really be the rare combination of person and artist that English literature is so rich in. Still, despite everything, Rilke's poetry is the greatest in Germany since Goethe and Hölderlin. His importance will only grow, as the issue of how to re-create humanity in Germany becomes a live question. The perfume of his poems, a bit redolent of the salon, must be allowed to dissipate. Maybe time will help remove the smell too.

In the last two weeks I've written a number of sonnets, seven, and a three-stanza poem. It seemed to flow from my pen. And I thought I'd never write again. The

57. The Platonic notion that abstractions or immaterial ideas truly exist before, or independent of, particular things.

creative process is impossible to understand. It is the opposite of consciousness. The other side of the coin. Beware the false [*word missing*] of consciousness.

## Wednesday 9/12 [58]

There are times when I'm completely certain that Gertrud and the child are one of the seeds waiting inside me. I can see their faces before me, almost bringing tears to my eyes. What I've been through with Hanna fades, pales. The feeling has become more remote because of the poems, where I tried to blend a lot from me and a lot from her. To the extent that I realize how much it changed me to be with her, I'm sure it wasn't all just literature. Otherwise it would have disappeared without a trace, leaving only little verses, nothing more. As it is, it included everything. I always had to commit completely. All of a sudden I see Gertrud in a different light. Maybe life with her will be more bearable now. My endless irritability will subside, maybe.

Painful thoughts about after the liberation. Will the Dutch have kept their good qualities: their public integrity, their tendency to judge each case individually? Or will they come out "changed." The English are just outside Holland.

It's strange how little it all has to do with me, fundamentally—how all my efforts are directed inward,

58. Tuesday 9/12 or Wednesday 9/13.

at thoughts, relationships between people, poems, experiences. Intense longing for Gertrud and the child. And often for my parents. I talk to them sometimes. Oh, much too late!—

**Saturday 9/23**

Last night, for the first time, I was no longer afraid of Rilke's poems. I can read them with an inner peace, without any fear of unlearning my own music. My poems can stand up to them—not in defiance, but in the calm certainty that a strong and lasting tone of their own sounds in some of them (sonnets!). I feel closer to Rilke now that I'm more removed. I respect his extraordinary accomplishment all the more, e.g. the superb lines in the *Sonnets to Orpheus*. (9th. 26th.)

What will happen with my own cycle of poems, I often wonder, in amazement. There are 29 of them now. Including some that are successful, no question.

*Dream.* I walk into a whitewashed church, Gothic, crowded, push my way through the packed center nave until I'm standing almost right in front of the altar, which has two burning candles on it. Suddenly the organ starts playing. A church concert!, I think, and then a singer steps right in front of me and starts singing. Oh, it's Jouke Cup., I think,[59] so this is the concert she told

59. Oratorio singer Jouk(e) Couperus.

me about. I can't tell whether she sees me. She looks like a different woman, she's wearing her hair the way Gertrud used to. She sings full of feeling, bizarrely, and already by the first measures she is moving her body to the music in a strange way, more as if she were on stage than in a church concert. She stamps her feet. People start to laugh. And then she sings the same phrase over and over again, with the same movement each time, getting more and more exaggerated, and she cries: "Yes, that's how I sing it, that's how I learned it, that's how it has to be." First it sounds triumphant, then weaker and weaker, while she goes more and more berserk trying to prevail. Finally she collapses onto the stone floor, loudly wailing and moaning. People don't know whether to laugh or not. I jump up, run over to this face contorted in pain, beside itself, with big eyes (Gertrud's!), and I say—and the whole church can go to hell: "But Jouke, it's me, Hans, look at me. Your singing was so beautiful, and it had to be that way, with that phrasing. No one else knows how beautifully you can sing." Full of love, I embrace the helpless creature, I understand that she has had a severe attack, but also that she can and will continue singing. The way I've always pictured a man being there for a woman in time of need—that was how I was with her. I encouraged her, took her hand as I talked. She could feel, in my closeness, that I felt only love, no lust. She slowly regained control of herself, calmed down, and squeezed my hand. Finally she walked farther into the church, which was emptier now, and sang some more. It was radiantly beautiful. I loved the pain and trauma I felt behind her song. But knowing that it was me who had brought her back—that meant everything to me. It wasn't just vanity about a successful treatment.

All sorts of things come to mind about this dream: First, Jouke, who got stuck when she was singing with Marie.[60] Gertrud's dream about herself and the child.[61] Gertrud's career, her life. That you could learn from Bonhoeffer how to handle the insane.[62] My love for Gertrud. My desire to be with her, and the strong feeling I often have of her helplessness. My fierce battle against my own sadistic tendencies. This dream came after a short, severe fever and intestinal sickness, preceded by a short, severe psychological shock when Hanna told me about sleeping in the same room with her sisters, how they acted with each other. I suddenly saw the three girls before my eyes, in their little nightgowns, with their girlish fears, very moving. I was devastated. Hanna didn't notice anything. It's the same battle I so often

60. Marie de Monchy, a pianist and piano teacher with whom Keilson also played music during the early years of the war.

61. See 6/18, p. 48.

62. Keilson had studied with Karl Bonhoeffer (1868–1948), an eminent professor of psychiatry and neurology, in Berlin.

have to fight with her. And a signpost pointing the way was in the dream!—

Meanwhile, heavy fighting in the Netherlands! Nijmegen, Arnhem![63] These events, however much they grip me, are no longer my real life. Only a virtuous tribute paid to society. Then there's the other, main life—the human being, the poem, people together.

Played Bach with Cora van der Lek and him.[64] Rediscovered Mozart last week, the Kegelstatt Trio.

Even in flipping through them—number XL[65]—it hits me that if these poems (the sonnets) are ever printed and someone else picks them up, who knows if they will be able to grasp this great struggle for clarity of heart. When I just read it, it seemed to me that the existential

63. In Operation Market Garden (September 17–25), the Allies made unprecedented use of airborne forces—gliders and paratroopers—to try to secure bridges in Nijmegen and Arnhem and advance north across the Waal and Lower Rhine Rivers; the fighting came to be known as the Battle of Arnhem, which ended in a major defeat for the British army. On September 22, "Black Friday," the Germans inflicted heavy casualties on the British outpost north of the Rhine, and the defeated Allies withdrew on September 25.

64. Probably Jan van der Lek, Cora's husband and Leo Rientsma's neighbor and coworker, who played the flute.

65. The "L" was added later; it is not known when the sonnets were numbered as they are in the typescript. Sonnet X is addressed to Death; Sonnet XL, too, is thematically related to Keilson's later novel *The Death of the Adversary*.

side of the poems, the purely—for me—personal side, is almost as important as the aesthetic side. I am trying to become a human being through them.

I've just now consciously realized what my calmness about the great battle looming in the Netherlands is: Gertrud's last dream image![66] It's almost certain!

**10/2/44.** It's that my nature always forces me to go to extremes, and to bring someone else along with me. It happened again with Hanna. Concentrating on the spiritualized object of my poems alienated me from the living subject herself. She realizes it, feels the coldness when we're together—recently. Only my instinct to shut down my consciousness, where there is no place for other people and being considerate, lets us be close. For me it is an addiction to an intoxicating drug. And then, when I see what I've done, my heart wakes up. Pity, shame, I'm moved—and I start to feel a genuine deep feeling of attraction and love. These detours! And it doesn't help, she clings even harder the more I humiliate her. Today I had to bring my violin when I came to see her, since I had nothing to say after the last time we were together. She realized, and cried while I played. This deep, bitter wound, almost like pleasure, at making another person suffer. For the other person it's suffering, for me a sickness! And still, even now, the girlishness

66. See 6/18, p. 48.

when she throws herself into my arms and stammers my name like a drowning woman. I'm not so rotten yet that I can't feel ashamed!

And meanwhile all the destruction of the cities. Holland is being damaged so badly. And how long will it last? Always, always I'm thinking of Gertrud and the child. This pain is what underlies the excesses.

But I'm not fooling myself, I am shocked too, struck by sounds and colors I used to be deaf and blind to. The conflict grows and grows: to write or to live. The extraordinary excitement and the mercilessness. Being ruled by drives that you'd very much like to think are outside of you but that find a home in your own breast after all—only they're hidden for a long time, secret, and suddenly they burst out with a will of their own. Not that that makes you any less responsible. Which I mean not in the moral sense, but in the sense that your life is answerable to something bigger than you, outside of you.

**Monday 10/8.** It's good to see feminine weaknesses (strong sympathies and antipathies, lack of objectivity, feminine motivations, jealousy, etc.) in an emancipated, masculine, academic woman (E. Bakker).

That from something inauthentic, something authentic can arise too. Confusions you feel caught in suddenly resolve into normal situations. Fears that muddy the picture the soul expects to see of its actions. And behind all the experimentation stands a shy person forcing herself to have courage for each next step, gradually learning to scorn pangs of conscience, since they are born of fear. Moral laws don't regulate our life with one another, they limit it. How much fear we are always pumped full of. I went looking for an animal and I found a human being. "I can't, what my husband does is his business but I have to stand firm, otherwise I'll have no right to complain later." I understood this and respected what she was saying. Still, I knew that a possibility was being cut off here, violently, cutting it off may have been very moral and admirable but still it diminished the self. I went around for two days and tried to make myself believe that I was a bastard. It was hard to do. So I stopped trying. Meanwhile there was regret from the other side, too, about a bite of food left uneaten. I learned how to wait without trembling. It was only too healthy, only too natural.—

A sword is hanging over our heads: that we will be randomly arrested and summarily shot over some real or imagined act of sabotage. This gives the day its transitory nature and gives every act an unintentional accent of expectation and completion. There is no more time to think things over. It's *Hic Rhodos, hic salta*.[67] Not with

67. Originally from Aesop's fable of an athlete who boasted that he had once jumped an amazing distance in Rhodes. A skeptical bystander says, "Rhodes is right here—jump here." In other

any sense of excitement—but who knows how it would feel to face the firing squad. I'd try to save myself to the very last moment. Make any compromise. I have to, if it'll give me the chance to see the end with my own eyes. I still have no respect at all for so-called heroic deaths. "Life is not the highest good":[68] an idiotic "ideal-istic" sentiment, proclaiming something just for the sake of striking a glorious pose. I want to live my life to the end, see how far it can go and by what means. You can serve the spirit only while you're alive, find immate-rial content only in material form. How could it be other-wise? The immaterial cannot be grasped—it is immaterial. It must be given form.

Saw a reading of *Hamlet*. What a play! Action and spirit. The Renaissance conflict is presented here and only "the living" can overcome it. Hamlet's mis-guided ideas about the doer and the deed. He confuses those who act out of passion with those who act from the intellect. His conflict is really between dreaming (letting it happen) and doing (making it happen). "Set-ting the world aright."[69] But he doesn't set it right. He

words: Put your money where your mouth is, let's see what you've got.

68. From Friedrich Schiller's *The Bride of Messina* (1803).

69. "The time is out of joint. O cursèd spite, / That ever I was born to set it right!" (act 1, scene 5). "To die, to sleep" is from the "To be, or not to be" soliloquy (act 3, scene 1).

only kills, puts to "sleep." He doesn't do something, i.e., bring to life.

### Saturday, 14th

It's in dealing with others that you discover who you are and learn what you're made of. The strongest argument there is against solitude. Now with Corrie too.[70] So easy and natural, joyful, tender. An education in being a man and a friend. A closeness almost free of lies. Unlearning fear. This is crucial for me: freedom from fear. How long it's taken to learn that. I can stay calmer when I think about my parents, how they might be dead. And I notice it playing the violin too: it is as though someone else is playing. Less harsh and vigorous, more delicate, more balanced. I discover new possibilities for the *piano* and the *cantilena*. Mozart Sonata in A Major. A long-standing dream. Good old Franz Hoffmann the first to learn it with me. Music is not only Orphic, it is also Apollonian. Mozart definitely. Beethoven, string quartet, penetrating intensity. And then equilibrium again.

I am reading Céline, *Journey to the End of the Night*. The mood of my first poems. Only greater, broader, more epic—which speaks against that. A negative, depressing book? Not in the least. Finally, a book without idealistic

70. Rosalina "Corrie" Groenteman, née Speijer (1902–87), in hiding with the Rienstmas.

window dressing. The courage it took to write a book like that! What lonely solitude. The urge to live. Not according to models, ideal examples. What a man this Céline was. And now an anti-Semite—a Nazi. How can he be so misguided? Does this drive to live warts and all, truly, with no false pathos, necessarily lead to the Nazis? Heidegger, too, and the young German nihilists, Jünger, Schauwecker, etc.[71]

The magnetic pull of the abyss, the sweet smell of death, the scent of putrefaction—all this is related to the insistent drive such books are born from. The desire to build expressing itself first in the desire to see one's cities, one's world, bombed into rubble (That way you can rebuild anew! More beautiful than ever before!!)[72]

I want to write a book like that about the Jews someday. Warts and all, with no Jehovahism, no messianic

71. Ernst Jünger (1895–1998), famous for his World War I novels *Storm of Steel* and *Fire and Blood* and for right-wing descriptions of Jews as a threat to Germany, though he declined official involvement with the Nazis; Franz Schauwecker (1890–1964), author of *Avenging Death: The German Soul in the World War* (1919), a colleague of Jünger's, and a self-declared Nazi.

72. This paraphrase is true to Nazi beliefs; it hardly matters whether Keilson was quoting a specific statement, for instance Hitler's "New Year's Proclamation" of 1944: "The bomb warfare against German cities profoundly moves all our hearts . . . but we will rebuild our cities to be more beautiful than they were before."

pathos. It must be possible. The opposite of Job. Not Dostoyevsky either. No anti-Semite could write such a book, only a Jew could do it. One of my plans that will keep me from becoming a doctor. Intense thought about whether it should be a first-person or third-person novel. It would have to show holiness, failed holiness, naked humanity, and life as such, existing alongside each other. The paradigmatic existential life. Most important: leave Heaven out of it, i.e. consider it in order to reject it. Otherwise it would be unbearable. Denying something which is—but which exists only in being denied, because only when a person says "No" can *it*, if it "is," say "Yes" with its being. That is its self-legitimation. A human being's "Yes" is a farce, it seems to create something when in fact the thing was there already. "Truth is the same for angels, humans, and demons."

**Wednesday. October 18.** A dog peeing in the room whenever someone plays the flute. Something yellow, with a burnt smell, referred to as pudding. He read the reports from the English radio: slowly, nasally, a little singsong. Mass murders in Polish concentration camps. For Christmas the English have more turkeys, fish, marmalade—one thing after another, enjoy. He gave a loud yawn, ha ha, ha. Well, they wanted to be happy again.

Thinking: we just have to endure it. The mass murders in Poland too. Just carry on. The way a general thinks, with his soldiers, when it's going to bring us closer to liberation—but those poor wretches, doomed to be slaughtered. You feel all puffed up inside, like a pig's bladder. What does it really matter that you're alive here while thousands and thousands are dying over there.

But what must they be thinking, the moment they're led into the gas chamber. They say Poles but they mean Jews. We should take Jewish children when they're still young and build up their immunity with small doses of gas, the Jewish state should, for the next pogrom! But who knows, the goyim will probably just use electricity then. And here we are, with all our talents!

Maybe it's only out of despair that a good deed—something honest, free of all vanity and desire for recognition and respect—can come. I signed up with the Red Cross. I won't be sent to the front, which is what I actually hoped for and was afraid of at the same time. Just to the Bethel hospital. But still, the only true and genuine thing I've done in a long time (I also wanted a piece of paper that would give me a little protection from the razzias, but no one needs to know that). Something to escape from all the garbage here—my own trash, poems, etc. Sex. But only Bethel hospital!

Céline, Céline, Céline—magnificent, he's so deeply in the thrall of his own daemon.

Read Wordsworth sonnets with Hanna. Again, deep bond with her. Can I tear this out of myself. But there's no use in any of it! Emotional connection, intimacy, or abandoning oneself to one's own garbage, who knows.

Interlude in Holland. The most important experiences in life, in the interlude! It's true, the genuine experiences come only in between, between the acts, and it's all a stage, an interlude between life and death. Everything: that this is not a place where history is being made, not a great power, just a little country. Before the curtain rises all the way and before it falls completely closed. The stage is not entirely darkened, the audience sits in a half-dark out of Rembrandt—half dream, half truth—everything is the interlude, the sober people and the passionate, criminals, scamps, Christians, Jews, émigrés, the Judenrat. (They *are* rats!)[73] Top hats on Passover. That was the Judenrat. They're dead and there's nothing good to say about them. To speak good of them would be an insult.

Someone who was a doctor, isn't one now, and will be one again, because he nurtures an intimate friendship with sickness. He pukes on the healthy, on the vanity of the healthy. A person becomes interesting only when he doesn't function anymore. Only a Christian woman.

A book full of gas, killing everyone who reads it.

73. The *Judenrat*, or Jewish councils, set up by the Germans to deliver set quotas of Jews for deportation, etc. Keilson uses the Dutch term, *Joodse Raad*, then puns on the German word *Rat* (council) with a parenthetical "*Unrat*" (filth, trash). The English pun with rodents is not a literal translation, but is close in spirit.

**Thursday. 19th.**   Decision: to work as a doctor. I need to talk to Verschuil[74] and Visser so that I'll be ready when I start at a hospital. The old tempestuousness returns. How is a person supposed to live, to be able to work, creatively?

I sleep more deeply now. Am free of all resentment for after the war. I want to work. But what about Gertrud, will I find my way back to her? Will I not be so irritated anymore at the kind of person she is—she's been through so many terrible things, and is still so full of surprises and tenderness. But how will I stand it. Not at the expense of my writing. A crazy problem. I see ever more clearly why I hit her—something I will never forget. I was too angry, I wanted her to be different. But

74. Everwijn Verschuyl (1903–97), a surgeon at Bethel hospital in Delft and company doctor at the factory where Leo Rientsma worked, the Netherlands Yeast and Spirit Factory (*Nederlandse Gist-en Spiritusfabriek*). A team at the factory was secretly working under the Occupation to isolate and produce the groundbreaking, lifesaving new drug from yeast, penicillin—an eighteen-month project completely independent of American and British efforts, with key information provided by a Jewish physician interned in Westerbork transit camp, Andries Querido. Verschuyl was the first doctor in the Netherlands to use penicillin on patients with serious infections; in April 1945, when the Germans allowed the Allies to drop food and medical supplies to help the starving and suffering Dutch, Verschuyl would be able to confirm that the chemical the Dutch had developed was indeed penicillin (www.dsm-sinochem.com/about-us/our-history/code-name -bacinol).

she doesn't understand quickly enough. And when she can't change she just pretends. Says horrible things, it's impossible to talk to her. Only after a blowup. Here I am angry again. She is too exhausting for my private life, there's no strength left for other things.—

I can't work on poetry anymore. But the harvest is not entirely brought in yet. I still hear the music within me, connected to the Hanna experience. An experience like that, never to become a woman! I expect and fear the worst, most of the time . . .

Conversations with the Bakkers about Germany. Trying to find an attitude that leaves open as many chances as possible for new relations in the future. How hard it is to put aside feelings of hate and revenge so that it's possible to imagine and understand the future. The Germans have made themselves hated, that's undeniable. It's wrong to act as though nothing has happened. They have too much to answer for. Forgive and forget?—no, but not "unto the sixth generation" either.[75] That would be just as nonsensical. Hitler's proclamation to the German people: Let yourself be wiped out, and help make it happen.[76] Maybe there's no need for any post-

75. A reference to God visiting the iniquity of the fathers on even the third and fourth generations (Exodus 34:6–7 and elsewhere in the Bible).

76. Long after it was clear that Germany had lost the war, Hitler continued to fight, a decision that cost millions of lives.

war plans at all, since there won't be any Germans left. So then who will read my poems, perform the operas and plays? A terrible problem.—

German policeman: But we're not bad people!

Where do the battle lines run? Herr Schäfer: Because they're so long and the car is so small. This way you'll get it back.

Leo lay outstretched on the floor, drilling holes in the evacuation crates for the guinea pigs! Like an Arab at midday prayer, on the floor.

The three Sanders girls, dancing around the room in their nightgowns and crawling under the covers at bedtime, I can see little Hanna. Happy, playful, attractive in that way I can feel down to the roots of my being. And it wakens in me a mood addicted to suffering and to causing suffering. An ambiguous back and forth, it makes my jaw tense. I could take her in my arms and crush her.—

Swaneveld. The ultimate war profiteer, with white gloves but at the same time raking it in on all sides. His being hard of hearing is his main source of income.

---

Nearly half of Germany's military casualties and countless civilian deaths came in the last ten months of the war. At the very end, Hitler would explicitly call for the self-destruction of Germany, for instance in the so-called Nero Decree of March 19, 1945, which ordered that all German infrastructure be demolished to prevent it from being used by the conquering Allies.

A moral bastard! "And then I'll give a doctor 1,000 marks to patch up my wife, Sophie"! That's how he sees nature! After an abortion. And she was so happy she was pregnant. But still: Business considerations! The only valid reason there is, for moral bastards. "I didn't want a child because I was afraid word might get around."

Hallauer,[77] that pimp, hit my weak point. Going to school and letting Gertrud work. And with that he set me on a fateful path that I'd have preferred to avoid. The devil in my life—a gray-haired gynecologist. Devil of misfortune! Is he still alive? It took years for me to get free of that.

Life in Germany: A life that kicks you in the ass. You build calluses there, but unfortunately that's the wrong place for them. In Holland the callus slowly goes away. And that hurts too.

Mrs. [*illegible*], brunette, menopause problems. A slim delicate little face, and you can read in it the battle between mockery, sensuality, and the Catholic Church. Synthesis: secretary, Red Cross. And maybe not without

77. Benno Hallauer (1880–1943), a gynecologist, often mentioned as "Uncle Benno" in prewar letters from Keilson's parents in Berlin. Keilson calls him "the good Benno" in letters to Gertrud, and he seems to have helped Gertrud convince, or trick, Keilson into fleeing Germany for the Netherlands (see *My House*, ch. 17). Nothing is known about the incident referred to here.

significance for my future life, having set me on my path to become a doctor.

**Saturday. 10/21.** Eydtkuhnen has fallen! My father's birthplace![78] Is he still alive to hear the news? Invisible, tormenting despair. Almost numbed. Oriented to daily life and nothing else. At night with Corrie, understood what it means to have your children taken away.[79] A horror that nothing will ever be able to make up for. One cannot, must not forget. To act as though nothing had happened would be the same crime.

Read Petrarch poems for the first time. What subtlety, lightness with all their beautiful depths. He is surely someone who lived on the surface and kept his depths only for his poems. I know how that is! But what poetry! Not worthy of imitation.

"I really trust you," Corrie said. "You should," I answered. And at the time I believed it myself. But it seems like everyone betrays everyone. "Betrayed," what does that even mean. That my energies are directed at many things? All I can do is try to be entirely there for someone

78. Eydtkuhnen, called Eydtkau between 1938 and 1945, now Chernyshevskoye in Russia, on the border with Lithuania.

79. Corrie had three children with Emanuel Groenteman. The older two, Esther (b. 1923) and Abraham (b. 1924), were deported and killed at Auschwitz; Sonja (b. 1938), the "little girl" mentioned below on 10/24, survived.

at the moment when I'm with them. No unpleasantness, no secrecy, just—lust. Below the waist gets short shrift. The voracious desire to know, which drives a person to act out. Right to the edge. Wanting to know—not only from the box seats, but in the action, onstage. There is a lustfulness in thinking that drives a person to new life experiences, irrespective of what kind. You could say: a hunger. I am firmly in its grip. The slowness and caution of the people here is a way of limping along behind life. And yet it's a nice life! Boredom, the essence that underlies any continued existence.

Hannetje[80] yawned the first time, after 45 minutes of work. Out of practice!

No mail from Gertrud today. Very anxious. Almost out of my mind. Constantly imagining her body, which I used to like so much, and her caresses, which I haven't liked very much recently. She doesn't have the sensitive delicacy that excites me the most. You can't ignore your own sensuality. A Hebbel conflict, almost. Only no Christine Enghaus.[81] But she might show up, and then it would happen. Or a musical woman. I would be lost.

80. Hannie, the younger Rientsma daughter. Keilson was apparently working with her as a kind of tutor.

81. Friedrich Hebbel (see note 2, p. 3) married Enghaus, a beautiful, wealthy actress, abandoning the mother of his children, the self-sacrificing Elise Lensing, who remained faithful to him until her death. Hebbel felt that "a man's first duty is to the most powerful force within him, that which alone can give him happiness

This knowledge makes the ground unsteady beneath my feet. Aside from that she could be less talented. I've changed my mind about women, just like about the weather. No more accomplished women, just give me a warm, vivacious human being, musical, someone who doesn't read a book while you're playing music. Oh, Dadaut. I am so distant from you, yet I totally understand you. I am so different now since we've been apart. As if it will have to stay this way forever. Maybe she has an intuition about all this but she's not strong enough to bear it. Hence her outbursts of rage. I want to learn to endure them.

Talked to Corrie last night about Gertrud too. It gave me a very warm, intimate feeling. Still, the great split in me remains. Not only in her nature. But in the way I respond to it.

**10/23.** The premature news of Breda's liberation[82] brought out a pessimist's (Co's) pessimism. And so when he said that it would take at least another two months, people complained he was ruining the mood. Later, it turned out to be premature. The pessimist, under pressure from the others, had turned into an optimist and

---

and be of service to the world," in his case his creative gifts, which "the miserable struggle for existence" would have destroyed.

82. See note 52, p. 57, on Mad Tuesday. Breda, in the southern Netherlands, would eventually be liberated on October 29.

forced himself to believe that it would take two weeks at most. Then, when everyone was depressed, including our pessimist-turned-optimist-against-his-will going around in a bad mood with a scowl on his face, the others ganged up on him again, for being dumb enough to think it would only take two more weeks and sitting around writhing like a worm now that it was taking longer. Fate!

He was an artist—with corns! Sensitive. Stepping on his toes awakened the most sublime sensations.

It's lasting too long. The war. One night, heard uninterrupted thundering in the distance. The ground shook. Artillery? Airplanes? A strange, titillating thrill, not unpleasant, witnessing danger from a safe distance. Then, when V-1s were launched right near us last night, it was different. Still, I felt no panic. Sympathy, willingness to go along with anything that might happen.

The morning torpor I've felt for years, even as a child I think. I remember only a few isolated exceptions, when I got up early with my father. He had to close the shades when the sun came up. The glorious feeling I had those mornings, all alone on the warm, still-empty streets. The bliss I felt going to school on those days.

**Tuesday. 24th.** Corrie says: "You'll think this is dumb, but Christians pee more than Jews. When I was in Zaandam, well, the man went to the bathroom 5 times a night. I was sleeping downstairs on the sofa and heard him whenever he walked by. I slept badly. He left the door open.— And here too. She's already gone to the bathroom 7 times today. I don't think they wash their hands."

News from Buskens.[83] The Canadians swam across a 25-foot antitank trench. But two days later the city was back in German hands.—

An unpoetic life. Musical though. The reality of things never reveals itself as reality. It is only matter, a chemical object. But the moment we grasp something, we bring to it something of ourselves: brilliance or dullness. The Dutch are down-to-earth because they want to reach an agreement, find common ground with a partner that leaves open the possibility of being fair to both parties. That can only happen when both sides eliminate everything personal. What's left are their interests. This is not usually a process that can grasp "reality"—which is much richer in imagination, more colorful, more personal.

Letter from Gertrud that really hit me. I'm starting to react to her letters differently. Less blustering, calmer. More supportive than before, maybe. She is constantly

83. Probably pastor and theologian Jan Buskes (1899–1980), active in the resistance, to whom Keilson wrote a thank-you letter after the war.

meeting people in her life she is far superior to, but who still have to flaunt their power over her. Like the Gülchers.[84] People are so afraid! If it really was the way she said in her letter, then she was entirely in the right. I just worry that the excitement is too much for her. And wears her down. I wrote her back a long and detailed letter. I hope I found the right tone, the one she needs right now.—

The Russians are 30 km into East Prussia. This offensive will be decisive. The English and Americans are dawdling too long, not going anywhere; the Russians have more oomph. Apparently they conduct the war more imaginatively too. The English have started an offensive against Den Bosch.[85] How far will they get?

What will happen to the Jews when this war is over? My discussion with Verschuyl made me think of Prague, where the Jews face as many anti-Semitic demonstrations as anti-German ones. He, too, used me to air his anti-German feelings at first. Later, when he realized he was in the wrong, he made an about-face.

But what about me personally? Which nationality? Be a doctor? Go back to school? Exams? Surely not that.

84. A family in Hilversum, near Naarden and Bussum, where Gertrud found work as a housekeeper for a time after Keilson went into hiding.

85. Den Bosch, or 's-Hertogenbosch, is another city in the southern Netherlands; the English offense was successful and the city was liberated.

Will they give us citizenship in Palestine? And then what? Plant orange trees? A chicken farm? Not me. I'd rather stay here as a writer. Or get a job at Bijenkorff.[86] Or take exams to be a psychological counselor. But I will be a doctor, even if it's in Russia! Or Sweden. Norway. I'll do whatever I have to do. Give it my all, everything I can do. Maybe it'll be enough. Whatever happens, I don't want Gertrud to have to work. I'll try to get money from Goudsmit, Landshoff, Bermann-Fischer, New Society of History, Het Joodse Comitee.[87] I'll make whatever money I can so that I can work 3–5 years in peace. From the Völkerbund. From anybody. First get my doctorate. I can't count on my sister Hilde. To get money for me in Palestine. Book advances! That doesn't make you rich. I have two short manuscripts: *The Death of the Enemy* and *The Laundry Tag, or,*

86. De Bijenkorf is a large department store in Amsterdam that reportedly had its own psychological counseling department.

87. Alfred Goudsmit (1886–1973) was the head of De Bijenkorf, founded by his father; after the war, he became a founding member with Keilson of L'Ezrat Ha-Yeled (Children's Aid or "To Help the Child"), the first organization for the care of Jewish orphans who had survived the Holocaust. Fritz Landshoff (1901–88) was the head of the German-émigré division of the Dutch publishing house Querido from 1933 until it was shut down in 1940. Gottfried Bermann Fischer (1897–1995) succeeded his father-in-law, Samuel Fischer, as the head of Fischer Verlag, which had published Keilson's first novel, *Life Goes On*, in 1933.

*In Hiding.*[88] Maybe they'll be translated. The novella, *In Hiding*, can maybe be used as a film script. A feature film with a documentary aspect. Leonhard Frank's *Carl and Anna* was a short book too, but still powerful.[89] What's behind this hunger for money is my fear of being cast out into terrible poverty again with wife and child, entirely dependent on chance. Especially because of Gertrud's health. Wanting to have a more or less bearable private life. The ideal: Own property! A monthly income that you can count on, can know in advance. Until I have a solid foundation as a medical doctor. 3–4 years at least. Who knows. Until then I can maybe get some stipends.

Exhaustion between Hanna and me. When there are too few secrets between people. I have the feeling of having sucked everything out of her it's possible to get, like out of a lemon . . . and then turned it into poetry. An unethical undertaking. Almost totally unacceptable,

88. These became *The Death of the Adversary*, published in 1959, and *Comedy in a Minor Key*, published by Querido in 1947. Hanna Sanders's Dutch translation of *Comedy in a Minor Key*, probably finished while she was still in hiding, was also published in 1947, by Phoenix Books in Bussum.

89. Leonhard Frank (1882–1961), a dissident and émigré German writer, whose most famous novel, *Carl and Anna* (1926), was made into the MGM movie *Desire Me*, starring Robert Mitchum, in 1947.

morally speaking, unless you take the quality of the new creation as compensation for what's been lost. If someone did that to my own daughter, what would I think? Would I be a little depressed? I'd wish she had put up more resistance. When I think how strongly I fought, to the bitter end, not to let it degenerate into just a fling. *Je ne peux pas aujourd'hui.* And now not quite enough mystery. Tired. How on earth was Shakespeare able to write his countless sonnets about it? And Petrarch? Was their experience more superficial, or was it deeper? Were they greater artists? Did their nervous systems work differently? Who can tell. What I know for sure is that I dived down to the very core of my existence in these poems.

I'm still in the grip of the prose story I want to write about Sara Klatzkin in the hospital. The police officer's story.[90] If I only knew the right frame it would be easier. Should the policeman be the narrator, or should I narrate it myself as something heard from him? Increasingly leaning toward the latter. It makes for easier transitions, more suspense, nuances, juxtapositions, more possibilities than simply the normal story.— Thanks to Céline I'm pumped full of dynamite again for fiction. It's an extraordinary book, whether for the ages or not doesn't matter. A new mysticism, no realism at all, everything

90. See July 15, p. 54, about Police Inspector W.

both internal and external seen with a mystical bringing-to-life. Even sexual things are not described for their own sake, they add color to the expressive quality of the events. Almost an ontology.

Talk with Corrie. It is embarrassing to see a person's limits too often, and even more embarrassing when you see someone calmly bearing up under, even standing above, the boundaries drawn for them. Corrie endures Suus's and Leo's limits remarkably well. She can tell that they don't like having her at the table, or in the living room at all. She is sensitive. Too sensitive for her almost primitive, common nature. And she's picking up on some-thing true. It really is that way. People just don't know how to talk with someone so far beneath them. Well, they did with Hendrik,[91] but he was more intellectual. She sees it, feels it, suffers under it, and bears up with a smile. She does the laundry during the day, it's done by 4, and then she sits all alone up in her cold room while Suus and the children sit in the warm living room and drink their tea. And it's nothing but stupidity in Suus, laziness, thoughtlessness. Corrie says, "I knew that when I started here, now I have to just stick it out, there's nothing else to do. There are bigger problems than this in the world. But then later I don't come down to the

91. Unknown, possibly someone else in hiding with the Rients-mas.

living room when they call me. I don't do it."— I tried to make her see that she probably should.

She told me: "Sometimes, when I'm just walking down the street, I think: Oh, you don't belong there at all.[92] When I hear Mrs. Rientsma walk singing across the room, I think: I will never, never be able to sing again." She gets overexcited, to the extent that that's possible for her. "What the krauts[93] did to me, to my children, do you understand." Yes, Corrie, I do. "My daughter was at the Schouwburg,[94] when she was being sent to Poland. She asked me to come with the little girl so she could see her one last time. I put Sonya in a baby carriage and went. A kraut was standing in front of the Schouwburg, rifle on his shoulder. He chased me off. I went down Kerkstraat with the baby carriage. Suddenly the little girl said: 'Mommy, don't look so mad, make a happy face.'" In all her misery, she told me how sweet her little girl was. Then they saw the older daughter one more time,

92. This sentence is written in Dutch.

93. Here and elsewhere, Keilson uses the Dutch word *mof*, a term for Germans going back to the Middle Ages but with the same derogatory associations in the World War II context as "kraut" in English.

94. A popular theater in Amsterdam, renamed "the Jewish Schouwburg" by the German occupiers in 1941 and repurposed in 1942 into a collection point for Jews being deported. Today a memorial stands on the site.

behind the bars. They were so happy! Children were playing in the inner courtyard, the little children, before they were sent away.

Suus asks me if I still feel like someone in hiding. I said that I do. She'd asked Corrie the same thing. Corrie said too that she never forgot her situation. And Suus was surprised! The evening after my conversation with Corrie, I asked Suus if, when she talked to me, she still thought about the fact that I have a wife and child. "No," she said, "I don't think of you as someone in hiding."

"And what about Corrie?"

At first she didn't understand what I meant. I was saying all this to try to make her realize Corrie's situation. "No, not Corrie either, there's absolutely no danger there," she said.

"That's not what I mean," I said. "I'm asking if, when you talk to her, you're aware that she has two children in Poland and a little six-year-old girl that she hasn't seen in almost two years."

"No," Suus said, "you asked me how I think about it—maybe it's not very nice, but I just see things my way."

"But I meant those other things," I said. She laughed; I winked. I'm very curious to see if this has any kind of result. Hardness of heart.[95]

95. *Die Trägheit des Herzens*, literally "laziness of heart," i.e., indifference to other people; this was the title of a much-read

She forgets that she took Corrie in as someone in hiding. For her, Corrie is first and foremost a maid. Hardness of heart. The issue here is not so much the evils of money as so-called education and culture! God-damn education, "higher" education! It makes the class question worse just as much as money does. Only Gertrud and Mrs. Goldsmit[96] were immune. Thank God, Gertrud too. I often think about Mrs. Goldsmit, when she came to see me in her short leather jacket with her hands in her pockets. A natural person! And Gertrud too. Thank God. Still, Corrie is better than her, in terms of pure humanity, and Suus is after all good in those terms too, innocently good. But what is a good deed, actually. From what soil does it spring? The whole complex of good thoughts and ideas with which you do justice to another person, does it need to be there? Can you see the other person in their whole humanity, or only in terms of a specific function? It's almost impossible to see them whole, in their full humanity, and yet that's what we have to do. Otherwise you get bogged down. The question of class is so closely tied to the function, the specific daemon or function of a human being. Here too. Or when Leo tells her how she should give

---

1909 novel by Jakob Wassermann about the foundling Caspar Hauser.

96. Probably Gertrude Goudsmit, the wife of the head of De Bijenkorf.

Hanna her bath.[97] It's practically a joke. While he doesn't notice if the children go without baths for a week. And Corrie pretends she needs his instructions, that she has to be told how to give a child a bath. Has he forgotten that she's given baths to children of her own?—

More than enough material for me, enough experience. Was with her. So relaxed, so free. More fire than there seems to be at first sight.

I think a lot about Gertrud. Deep longing. She really is right, you should treat your employees well, not only for their sake but for your own.

What is dinner conversation, really? Not just witty pleasantries but life in its fullness, with its sometimes witty, sometimes tragic moments, understandable to everyone.

Every Wednesday morning the hurdy-gurdy man rings the bell. To collect his money. He used to come and play, now he comes to get his money and the music is postponed until later.—

To forgive the Germans for their heinous crimes is impossible. Letting a man like Himmler come to power and giving him a free hand. I'm filled with overpowering rage a lot of the time: Wipe 'em out! The news of German cities reduced to rubble by the Russians gives me deep satisfaction.

97. Leo's daughter Hannie Rientsma.

News report on Radio Oranje about liberated Holland. Only when they crossed the border were the roads paved, and they said: "Boys, we're in Holland." Then they saw the first sign saying NO SOMETHING ALLOWED (I forget what), and they knew: We're home.— And then: Fewer skin problems, "our typical Dutch cleanliness"!! I couldn't help laughing. They wash the buildings and sidewalks here more than they wash themselves! I'd like to see some statistics about that.

**Sunday. 10/30.**[98]    The situation was resolved sooner than I'd expected. My conflict in the house was growing from day to day, especially with Suus, who didn't seem to notice anything. Leo becomes very withdrawn when anything rubs him the wrong way. One night, when we went up to Corrie's room after the lights went out, to turn on the little battery-operated emergency lamp, she was sitting there alone and rather desolate. Suus had invited her downstairs to the living room twice that evening. "It's fine if you come downstairs, you won't be in our way." Oops! That hurt. You'd have to be pretty unfeeling not to understand that. She lay in bed crying that night. I brought her some coffee. Before, when I was coming back from playing music, she had told me about this invitation. And that she'd declined.

98. Sunday was the 29th; the entry probably dates from Saturday, October 28.

When Leo and I were alone, I told him Corrie was crying in her bed.

"Oh, you mean because she feels so isolated here?" He understood it at once.

When Suus came in, the conversation stopped. Then he told her.

"Why?" she asked. "Any particular reason?" Her bad conscience was speaking. And also in what she said next, which I can't recall anymore. "She doesn't feel like she belongs here," Suus said, "and if you ask me she's absolutely right." That hurt. Pow.

I stayed calm and didn't get angry. Suus vented all her social resentments, which weighed heavily on her, nothing but class resentment. All while there was a woman crying upstairs with her children in Poland, her home life torn apart, her family destroyed. He was visibly embarrassed. I stayed calm and told them about Gertrud's job with Spier.[99] Without keeping anything back. My attitude was: They just have to be taught the understanding they lack. And I stayed calm. Only fear makes a person rude. I wasn't afraid anymore, so I could be polite. But Suus kept hammering away at the differ-

99. Julius Spier (1887–1942), a chiropractor and student of Jung's who had a small practice in Berlin and then in Amsterdam. It is not known when Gertrud worked for him and in what capacity. Keilson's posthumous papers contained a typescript copy in German of Spier's posthumously published 1944 book, *The Hands of Children*.

ence. Until he said: "Of course she feels isolated. If we try a little, we can change that." She stayed stubborn and spiteful.

Finally she burst out, the first time she ever had at me: "Corrie doesn't try either, she always lays the tablecloth a way I don't like, and how she makes the beds too!" The domestic order had been disturbed, unleashing rancor. What a difference—upstairs a woman who's lost everything, maybe including her two oldest children, and here a woman in a tizzy about her sheets and tablecloths. History turning into farce once again!

I reassured her and offered to help straighten out the situation. The next day, I wondered if I should talk to her about having said Corrie "wouldn't be in the way." I decided not to, since I wasn't trying to hand out punishments or rewards. Besides, that really would have disturbed the peace between the two women. But Suus said maybe Corrie was crying because she's thinking about her little girl? People are so happy when they can clutch at an acceptable, plausible lie! I promised to look into it.

**Tuesday. 11/30.**[100]   Sitting reading with Hannie. She reads haltingly, badly. Prefers to read silently to herself. Suddenly the word *witch* comes up—the Witch of Endor. She asks me about it. I tell her that there was a king who

100. A mistake for 10/30, which was a Monday.

was going to war and he wanted to know if he was going to win, so he went to the witch who lived in a place called Endor. "And where did you read that?" I asked her. In the Bible. "What kind of book is that?" A book with stories. "What kinds of stories? Like Minette and the Cat Prince?" No, not silly stories like that. "So, what kind?" No answer.

"Well," I say, "they're stories about kings and other men." Tears are already starting to come to her eyes. Suddenly, just so that she can say something too, Suus says: "About our Lord, about God! You know that!"[101] Hannie nods. Pow! It's happened.

"Who is that?" I ask. No answer. I ask again, because I don't like working with concepts that no child can understand. Hannie goes out of the room, to clean her glasses. Comes back in. After she tells me that her glasses were dirty, I ask her again. She seems to have calmed down. When I ask about God again, she bursts into tears, turns red in the face, coughing. I think she's choking. A real fit, she must also be scared of not being able to answer. I call Suus in and show her the screaming child. She's terribly shocked and takes her into the other room.

Was it God that struck her down with this fit? Or actually this concept that she couldn't grasp, that could

101. This sentence is in Dutch: *Van onze Lieve Heer, van God, je weet wel.*

only awaken primal emotional complexes of fear, terror, and disgust? Was it just my persistent questioning, or just my questions plus her not liking to read out loud? Or is the God complex so ingrained that it pulls everything else into its orbit? The child is surely predisposed, pre-destined in a way, to experiences of fear and anxiety. So then don't use concepts whose emotional content is too difficult and powerful, and that have no imaginative content that her consciousness can feed on!

I wonder how Suus will twist this around. It would be better if she left the child alone with me when I'm working with her. "I thought your explanation was so strange: 'stories about kings and other men'!" Instead of waiting to see what I was planning to say next. And especially not this "You know that"!! Bah. No religious education and then "About God! You know that, child!" I was wrong. Suus doesn't have the faintest idea about child-rearing! My own approach was 50% backward. And yet it was right.

On Friday I ran into Mrs. Goudeket[102] at the tram stop in The Hague. I recognized her at once, even though she looks much older. But a fine, noble face.

---

102. The Dutch author Marianne Philips (1888–1951), who was married to the trade unionist Sam Goudeket (1886–1979). The couple lived for a time in Bussum and helped bring Keilson's parents to the Netherlands.

"I'm amazed you recognized me, everyone tells me I've gotten so gray."

"I've been thinking about you for two weeks straight," I answer. "I've been trying to get in touch with you." Which is true. She was happy to hear it. And let a tram go by so that she could take the next one with me. "Maybe we could see each other very soon."

"Yes," she said, "I'd like that. I'd like that." We got on the tram.

"Maybe I could come see you."

"Or I could come see you."

Silence.

"I have to ask my people if that's okay," I said, a bit sheepishly.

"Me too," she said.

Something snaps between us. The happy anticipation is gone. It's crazy.

She tells me about her husband, her children. Shows me photographs. "Maybe we could meet in some neutral place," I suggest.

She refuses: "Let's forget it. I'd rather not. I'll write to Gertrud, or—"

I didn't say: "But I need to talk to you." I didn't push it. I could have made it happen. But I was so struck by this relapse into caution, from eagerness into distance. I let it go.

She was still in a good mood. I asked her if she's been

able to work. She told me about two or three manuscripts she'd had to burn, because she had to evacuate
several times.[103] Said, rather loudly, that she was a bigger
pacifist than I am. And that there are atrocities on both
sides! I feel that I really need to talk with her. "This
nightmare is getting worse and worse," she said.

Maybe I spoke too intensely about my own work,
because she said, a bit miffed: "The publishers won't be
as eager after the war as you think." Now where did that
come from? Because she had had to burn her own
manuscripts? I couldn't help thinking of what Stefan
George said once: "I have cried all my tears in advance."
I feel the same way. But can other people understand that?

With Hanna yesterday. It's been a long time. It was
hard to come back to her. But her nature won me
over—unbelievably attractive, I'd never felt it like that
before. Afterward, deep depression and fear of the consequences. Saw how exhaustedly she slept. Even her
sleep is like a kind of floating, a wispy cloud over the
sea. If only I could grasp it, hold on to it. And all the
violence she calls up inside me. When I hold her in my
arms. It's her complete abandon too, which she expresses in everything, in her eyes, her body, her hands.
Something stirs within me, the desire to inflict pain,

103. "Evacuate" was a term used among the underground for
changing one's hiding place.

tenderly, I've never been aware of a feeling as mixed as this one.

I've known such hours with Gertrud too. Is the way back to her still open to me? I'm often afraid that Gertrud's nature, with so many things about it that annoy me, will tear me apart. In my mind's eye I see the following image: We're separated. She is waiting for me on the street, at night, walks up to me, and says in a soft, pleading voice: "Hans, it's our child. Barbara. She's very sick." "Our little Barbara," I repeat. And then I wait to see what I do next. A sentimental scene? Or stand my ground? Both possibilities are within me. Either way I'd suffer terribly. But Gertrud's voice, the way she can talk, so simple, so plaintive, like a pipe organ. It shakes me down to my innermost core. Whenever she's been like that, I was hers. My life was with her.

On closer inspection, Hannie actually gave the question "Who is God" an absolutely appropriate answer, namely howling, screaming, and throwing a tantrum. Fear, disgust, shuddering and wailing: that's what God is. It's just that Suus was too blind to see what she was doing, when she started by talking about "our dear Lord Jesus" without realizing what she was actually doing. "You know that!" That's not an explanation. She thought I was being strange when I described the Bible as stories about kings and other men. I pointed out that she, without realizing it, was avoiding the problem with an answer that seemed better but was actually worse, creating the instantaneous closeness that both destroys any authority and blocks any insight into what the other person knows. So this is good middle-class child-rearing!

Still, it's ridiculous, my feeling that she'd stepped on my toes. I completely lost my sense of proportion, the self-assurance that makes me strong.

Poor Gertrud.

**Wednesday. 31st.**[104]   Today, when I left the house (Wallerstraat) to go to Bethel, where Dr. Verschuyl was nice enough to let me assist at a few operations, and I was walking down a side street, cheerful, a little excited at the prospect, just before getting to Oude Delft, I saw myself walking down the street. It wasn't a hallucination, second sight, an out-of-body experience—it was a kind of deep consciousness of my own person. Not so much an inner presence becoming external, as something outside forcing its way in, and to hitherto unknown depths. A premonition become knowledge, you might say.

What I am is a schlemiel! Walking down the street, happy as a schoolboy, in an outwardly shabby raincoat, shoes worn flat at the heels and falling apart, a bum, and yet self-satisfied, in possession of nothing except Nothing, a wife and child, happy when I play a little music or when a poem works out—a schlemiel, a total failure across the board, except in one thing: Nothing! I felt all

104. Perhaps Wednesday, November 1.

of this without any hint of self-pity, that accursed, treacherous aftertaste of the weak in love with themselves. I thought back to my student years, the years studying medicine, when I needed to make money, all the things I missed out on, the things I lost without mourning them. A loss that is not mourned. So now I'm 35 years old,[105] and I've lived sometimes like a criminal, sometimes like a madman, and sometimes in a state of high tension, especially in the last few years, when I was writing more. A schlemiel. I felt I had truly reached my final state of being and that never in my life would I walk as lightly and easily as I was walking today.

I remembered my uncle, whose practice I was meant to take over, after which, if everything had gone well—as, luckily, it hasn't—I would have been a well-paid general practitioner at 25, i.e., buried alive. In Hamburg. Even then I toyed with the hope that something, anything, might come between me and this fate. And then this Something did come. Herr Hitler turns out to be this little difference, this Something!

I remembered, too, how I used to read about the lives of Verlaine, Baudelaire, Heine, Brentano, with the burning desire to do what they did. Not just the ambition to write poems like them, I mean, but more: the

105. Keilson would turn thirty-five in six weeks, on December 12, 1944.

readiness to make their sacrifice. In fact, I had no idea what this sacrifice was, I could only imagine what it meant, with whatever imagination and intelligence and ideas I had. In any case, I was too bogged down in my bourgeois life to be able to uproot this existence. All I had was the burning desire. And today, walking down the street to start being a doctor again, I suddenly knew for certain that my wish from back then had come true. Without my having noticed it, my life had been freed from all its artificial devices and prostheses; nothing was left but a small human being swimming in the void, pleased to realize that it was this void pouring water down his throat, and paddling like mad with arms and legs to get free of it. And yet linked to this element, his element. I had nothing left to wish for. Verlaine's pride as he lay in the hospital on his own bedsheets—his property—was mine too. I don't own much more than he did. Not inwardly either. It wasn't needed, none of it. I don't even have two sheets anymore. My ambition has vanished into thin air. That's how anyone who talks about me should see me. Finally, for once, with no persona. No mask.

And then the meeting with Verschuyl, this well-established surgeon only a few years older than me, and with those young students dreaming of a successful practice. I felt a little backsliding surge of jealousy of these carefree young people doing their medical work, cursing the Germans. My life was running its course somewhere else nearby, like a movie showing in the basement.

Still, the schlemiel in me quickly rose to the top again. I could only think about where this wondrous path I'm on will end, on which floor, or rather, which side-door that I intend to batter down this detour will lead me to. And thoughts of Gertrud, the woman sharing this path along which I became a father and a schlemiel. Also about the child, who will have to know that her father is a schlemiel.

My recent outbursts of greed and avarice and envy come from this ground that has disappeared out from under the schlemiel's feet: he quickly, secretly cuts himself a slice of bread from the loaf because he's terrified of starving. Not the hunger for power or possessions, but the hunger of the destitute.

That's what I'm writing my poems about, and poor little Hanna, who thinks I'm really somebody, too dumb to realize I'm a schlemiel. Or maybe she's so smart and kind that she doesn't let me see that she's realized it? She doesn't know whether my poems are true, or the extent to which they are just little word games by someone who is ultimately a "man of society." You don't know how true they are, I answer her. The truth is, only a schlemiel can write like that. A snob never can.

She still has the ideal of a knight in shining armor, maybe. And I, who wrote at the beginning that she was a mirror for me like I've never had before, have really and truly seen my reflection now, down to the last little gap in my rotting teeth. And I've let go of my vanity.

How useful these affairs are—but it's more than just an affair—for self-enlightenment. Enlightenment about life. When I'm with her it's almost impossible for me to forget, because I no longer have anything I need to forget. I've let go of every last little thing, kept nothing but the knowledge ringing in my ears: Schlemiel!—

Gertrud is going back.[106] Will it turn out well? I'm glad she has so much energy. Even if it destroys me. I will give her time to recover, then ask her to let me go. Her wanderlust is strong enough that she should be able to understand mine and let me go. How will this end? No one should be sacrificed. That's not necessary anymore. We're beyond tragedy. A schlemiel has nothing to do with any of that anymore. The fool sings in a comedy whatever the circumstances.—

The lyrical stream is gradually starting to flow again. Differently, more heavily. The hard, metallic tone is not as easy to get hold of as it used to be. But conscientious diligence is a good equivalent, one that it takes a schlemiel to recognize and make use of.

What will Mrs. Beer think of my poems?[107] She

106. To the house in Naarden, Van Halllaan 15, originally Gerd Klaaß and Traudelise Katz's, where Keilson, Gertrud, and Barbara would live after the war.

107. Emma Beer, née Longo (1882–1960), Evy Bakker's mother, was a native Italian, with whom Keilson discussed Leo-

understands something about these things. Will her morality let anything else in her have the floor? And will she understand the language?

**Friday.**   Corrie hears Cora call "Bram!"[108] and thinks of her own son Bram.

Conversation between Corrie and the director of the vocational school. You are the second wife? Not a Christian? He can't keep his mouth shut. It's bad. It is not bad in the least, but he'll never get anywhere in this line of work. He should become a salesman.

**Saturday. 3rd.**[109]   Despairing letter from Hanna. How much longer will I fool myself about her true inner state. A strong, combative letter, full of curses. She wants to tear herself free of me completely. She happened to overhear a conversation between Arie and me about Barbara and Gertrud. She can't stand having them competing with her anymore. She wants me all to herself. And wants me to put a quick end to the current situation.

---

pardi among others. Evy's father, Herman Beer, was in hiding with a false passport, like Keilson; Evy Bakker was thus "half-Jewish" herself, in Nazi terms.

108. Cora's son Bram van der Lek (1931–2013), later a Dutch politician, who in 2009 remembered vividly how seriously "Dr. van der Linden" took this thirteen-year-old's efforts at poetry.

109. Friday 11/3 or Saturday 11/4.

Of course she's right. I've cultivated an egotism of feelings for far too long—acting as though I didn't notice what was happening inside her. She's a girl, after all, and scared of being left empty-handed. She doesn't want to be nothing but the instrument on which I play my tunes. And here too I have to admit she is right. An unbending instinct made her write this. And since I know how horrible this all is, I've acted for a long time as though I didn't see or know. I want to tell her that, but then too she'll just look at me even more helplessly and say, "And?" She's had enough of literature.

She's right. Enough is enough. She wants to live. And then she doesn't know what she means to me. Just a fling? And afterward, nothing? This is something else I've entirely kept from her: that being with her has been a shock for me, such a blow to my life with Gertrud, a mortal blow, I'm afraid. A tremendous new perspective in my life—the possibility of marrying her and living differently than I've been able to with Gertrud, more peacefully on the inside. She doesn't know anything about that, and I can't tell her. Giving her even a slight glimpse into my life with Gertrud would shock her deeply. And encourage her to fight a fight that could turn very ugly.

But even in her aggression, her forcefulness, I love her very much. That small little head, so beautifully proportioned, wonderfully taut. I can't stop thinking about the strong, uninterrupted stream I heard when she was sitting on the toilet. For me, that too was a sign: of how everything about her is strong, taut, still young. It's glorious!

So she thinks that for me it's all literature—when there's so much more behind it. If she could take even a quick look into this diary, she would be less unhappy—but maybe emboldened. If she knew what connects me to her, she might feel more at peace—but might also have more hopes. I'm not only thinking about myself—but when I think about her and about how I could actually improve her situation, what I should do is simply play the brute and leave her. The last time she hugged me, after we'd been together, an expression came into her body and her eyes—something taut, tense, strong—and I was shocked, and I thought: something is tearing apart now, breaking in two. The way she bent her body. Strained to the utmost. Obviously this situation of having to sit around at Arie's doing nothing doesn't help. I saw all of that more or less clearly, at the beginning, but didn't act accordingly. Another voice showed me the other path. I'll try to talk with her a little today, tell her one or two things, that it's really not as conflict-free for me as she thinks. That it isn't just a fling or a literary experiment, but more, even if I don't talk about it that way. Does she really imagine that life afterward will simply pick up where it left off and go on as it was before? I often want to be with her more than I long to be with Gertrud and the child. Never in my life have I been able to forget myself the way I can with her. She is a danger to more than just Gertrud and the baby!— But it's time I show a little more respect for this girl who's entrusted me with all her affection, all her ardor. I can't change the situation, I can only make it easier to bear. And more kisses.

Rereading *Crime and Punishment*! What a glorious, wild and yet also controlled book. There is a great art to writing like that. Wrote two more poems myself. My concentration is failing, soon there'll be enough poems. And still, I want to keep working on them more.—

Ended up in a surprising conversation with Cora after reading her child's tests. Actually not that surprising. It started rolling when I asked what poetry she has in the house. Jan doesn't like poetry, and Cora used to write poems herself. Because of her experience with her father and Louis Somer, she can't bear the thought of "the artist's life."[110] She thinks that if that's what she's being robbed of, fine. Everyday life has its value too, and must be lived. Every kind of work has to be done well and an artist is nothing more than that. It startled me to hear about this struggle in this woman, where I didn't expected it. Well surely I'll be able to help her here. A

110. Cora van der Lek's father, Evert Temme (1881–1942), pursued various plans to improve the world throughout his life; Louis Somer (1901–66), with whom Cora had been engaged, was a Dutch violinist, conductor, and composer.

great uncertainty along with instinctive certainty, with respect to the children too. She is uncertain as a woman, not awakened. How many people there are running around with untapped possibilities, erotic and otherwise. I'll need to talk to her about that. It's the Thomas Mann problem, Tonio Kröger.[111] In this Friesland farm girl.[112]

**Tuesday 11/7.** I'd given Mrs. Beer my sonnets, in a sudden burst of wanting to break through the wall I've put up around myself with my secret writing and, even more, with this affair. We talked about them today. She said the same thing as Hanna, that you could feel a strange dichotomy in the poems: half of them are very heartfelt, the other half heartless, conscience-free. Not that that's meant in the dismissive sense as a criticism.

She thinks my poems are difficult. "But there's no doubt you're a poet," she said, giving me a deep and penetrating look with her bright ice-blue eyes. Not a

111. Thomas Mann was and remained a major influence on Keilson; as late as 2009, a 1950 letter from Mann was one of Keilson's prized possessions. The long story "Tonio Kröger" (1903), about the conflicts between art and love and the artist's alienation from everyday life, was especially important to him, as it was to the autobiographical hero of Keilson's first novel, *Life Goes On*.

112. Friesland is considered a backward part of the Netherlands, but Cora wasn't actually from there; she was also a drawing teacher's daughter, not a farm girl.

word about what occasioned the poems. Very delicate of her. Not even a tactful remark to acknowledge it. Then she said a few more things, partly in broken Dutch, more in fluent French, often in German. *La passion de la passion été.*[113]

She had more to say about several poems. Particular things they made her feel. She has an extraordinary understanding of how to read a poem. I could tell from her remark about the word "firmament" in the intimate poem [Sonnet VIII]. It's too weighty, she said, it almost breaks the mood. She is very nearly right. Although I felt a very deep satisfaction when she talked to me this way, with none of my excited vanity or embarrassed vanity, as on earlier occasions, which had often caused me some unpleasant self-introspection. I sat there while she, in her good, somewhat naive fashion—which is also very intelligent—showed me, in the language of gestures, where she sees my place in the hierarchy of poets. I was a little surprised at myself—at how sincerely calm I stayed in spite of the happiness she was giving me. Is this the result of the so-called *via dolorosa*, which makes a person indifferent to success and honor, or is it truly that what I care about now are the poems—the poem itself and not what I might achieve with it. The deep

113. The French is ungrammatical; it is impossible to tell exactly what Keilson heard or meant. Perhaps something like "Summer love is so passionate" or "in love with being in love."

chasm between what has become independent and has its own life, and that from which it came. The relationship between parents and children must be a little like that.

She asked me: Didn't I know that my poems were worth something? I answered that I only felt the extent to which a poem succeeded as a poem, and the extent to which it displayed failings or weaknesses. But even that you can never know. It's impossible to honestly say more than that about oneself. And that's true, that's what I think. My literary ambition, which used to aspire to being compared with poets like ——, is almost entirely gone. I just write, I leave literary criticism to others. I was amazed to find Wordsworth secretly competing with Milton. I can understand it as long as he lacked outward recognition, but what can have moved him—without question a major poet—to such senseless comparisons? Fear of being forgotten? The uncertainty of a genius who puts his faith in Nothing.[114] So to be a genius is it necessary to compare oneself to Milton? No,

114. Goethe's famous poem "Vanity! Vanity of Vanities!" begins with the line Keilson quotes: "I have put my faith in Nothing" (*Ich hab' meine Sach' auf Nichts gestellt*), a line that parodies in turn the hymn and Bach cantata "My all I to my God commend" (*Ich hab' mein' Sach' Gott heimgestellt*). Max Stirner (1806–56), philosopher of radical, anarchist individualism, made the line the title of the introduction to his 1844 magnum opus *The Ego and His Own*.

you can live on friendly terms with this Nothing, there is such a thing as a broken string that still makes music.

It seems to me that since I lost my fear of Rilke's poems I have laid aside this inner and outward vanity. I know that I am a poet and a schlemiel. I could dare to live like Verlaine or Achterberg—but that wouldn't be my life.[115] The tension—with, at the other pole, daily life and the needs of the day, the need to be normal and ordinary—brings with it an oscillation, anything but ordinary, whose pulse I can feel in myself. Not the one, *Poeta*, and not the other, upstanding citizen and doctor, but both: that's what I am, always undecided, now being one and seeking the other, now being the second and seeking the first. Staying anchored in one and, at the same time, feeling its limits, i.e. already including, in longing, the other too, which begins beyond these limits.

What a path, from the trembling, slimy greeting from Duinkerken[116] one day in A'dam in 1938 to today— is that what's known as development? Or is it just life, movement, change. Who knows how I'll feel about it tomorrow, maybe then I'll be in total turmoil again, but

115. On Achterberg, see note 4, p. 8, and note 20, p. 20.

116. Anton van Duinkerken (1903–68), a Dutch poet and the editor of *De Gemeenschap*, in which he published German poems by Hans Keilson between 1938 and 1940. Keilson once, in an emergency, had to spend the night at van Duinkerken's Amsterdam apartment.

at least there will always have been *once* when I was how I am today—I have tasted from this table once.

Mrs. Beer didn't actually dare say everything she thought.[117] When we parted I asked her to, saying I would be grateful for it. She interpreted that as a sign of friendship.

She told me about her friend, an Italian poet, whose poems handled different material. Still, she felt that his poems and mine were related in a way—in melody, intonation. "Is it the Old Testament pathos?" I asked. "Maybe. He's Jewish too." I thought that was very funny.

**Sunday. 11/12.** Felt what a lie really is. Disgust at one's own lie. A burden. And sadness. Desire for freedom. For an unspoiled state. The story with Arie and the vouchers I was taking to Kok's.[118] Even though I knew, I did it. So, Hans, what theory can help you now? You must have had some theory behind it? That in the end it doesn't matter who gets them. Everyone needs them— me too. I shared them with Corrie, trying in this way to

117. The text says she "did actually dare," but Keilson seems to have meant the opposite.
118. That is, was supposed to bring to Dr. Daan P. Kok in Delft, in the resistance. The ration coupons (Dutch *distributiebonnen*), for food and also clothes and tobacco, played an important role in the lives of those in hiding. Resistance groups raided city halls and distribution offices to acquire vouchers that they would then have to distribute to those who were keeping others in hiding.

lighten my fate . . . But the sadness remains—wanting to throw everything off my shoulders someday.

The lesson of *Crime and Punishment*. It does make my own life clearer. The fiery, feverish, stubborn side—and the secret struggle for salvation, for God. For being able to devote oneself to something. I was only able to do it once, with Hanna. Never with Gertrud. With her I have the ascent, the high flight, the rush of propulsion. Hanna just lets me be. But that's what I'm actually looking for. I don't go beyond my limits, I free myself from limits, from the arbitrariness of my upbringing, of circumstances.

Razzia in R'dam.[119] 40–50,000 men. Thousands spent the night in Delft. No fear when the rumor came that they might start here too. I'd just be a doctor in Passau or somewhere else in Southern Germany. My plan is firm. Lies and more lies. And suddenly you catch yourself at it after all. It's in your deepest core. Sadness. Sometimes you can beat the world only by lying. Otherwise, you'd bleed to death— outwardly. And so you hemorrhage and bleed internally. Inside yourself. And have the chance to transmute in silence the blood that has run and collected there into another kind of power. Metamorphosis. That is

119. The roundup in Rotterdam was not to find Jews but rather Dutch men between seventeen and forty, all of whom had been ordered to report for work duty in Germany.

the lie. How do you clean yourself off, afterward—when the misery comes.

Raskolnikov's punishment[120] is his inner torment, which he doesn't [*illegible*] with. His nature plays a trick on him. The theory permits murder, and the human being suffers. Raskolnikov's suffering is his one truth within his lie. He doesn't lie that. However much he masks it and playacts it. His suffering—behind it, he has nothing to say and only keeps suffering. Could someone write a book like that?

I had an idea today, when I was thinking about the possibility that I might get caught: A Jew in hiding has a fight with the people he is living with and voluntarily reports to go to Germany, as a doctor, under the name he has on his false passport. He goes back, to a small town, and experiences Germany's downfall. How he acts, his happiness at the defeat and the pain he feels about what is being destroyed along with it, the satisfaction of revenge, the pure animal suffering that rebels against death to the bitter end and refuses to die. A book like that would have great human possibilities. It would have to show everything: The Nazis, half-Nazis, quarter-Nazis, non-Nazis, anti-Nazis, the ignorant, the

120. Or "Raskolnikov's atonement." The title of the earlier German translation of *Crime and Punishment* means *Guilt and Atonement*. At the beginning of this diary's first entry, the two terms are translated "Guilt or atonement, crime or punishment" to keep both the literal meaning and the reference.

indifferent, the defeat-fanatics, everyone—and behind them all: Mozart! Schubert. The A Minor Quartet, or the D Minor. What a subject! But it would have to be suspenseful. Take place in a short span of time. I would love to write it. But first, the novel about Lea Klatzkin.[121] I just haven't found the form yet.—

Women! Yesterday Hanna was rebellious. She stared at me, with a look bursting forth from her tempestuous nature. She bent and tensed her body in tremendous inner tension. I watched her the same way I looked on the day before yesterday when someone was getting his leg amputated. I relished her torment. And even the dreadful accusations—that I see everything too objectively, why can't I just live? why am I always the intent observer? Today she almost apologized, said it was because she was in a bad mood yesterday. It made me like her even more than if she were all lovey-dovey and devoted and soft. That steely gaze, from her differently shaped, slightly squinting eyes. Wonderful. "Be like that more!" I wanted to shout. She thought I was mad at her. And almost apologized.

I am much more careful with her. I often see what I've done. When she's just sad and miserable. As she often is recently. I make a woman both things: very happy and very unhappy. Be warned! At the same time, the

121. See July 15 (p. 54) and October 24 (p. 89), where she is called Sara Klatzkin.

sight of her still moves me deeply. When I'm with her it's like I have entered a new clime. I hope I'll get to see her, later, when this time is over. The way she walks down the street. The bliss of a short evening walk. What waves of feeling crashing over us!— I feel so much gratitude to this woman who has tuned my breath to such poems.

**Thursday. 11/16.** Evening walk with Hanna. One of the most beautiful of our whole friendship. A girl has become a woman. She lay in my arms differently from how she used to. And then, a peculiar conversation about what she once told me: that she is unhappy. I struck a bit of a pose, saying that that wasn't exactly a compliment for a man, for a woman to tell him that he's made her unhappy. She realized that it was a pose and said so too. Then she suddenly asked me: "What do you think is the real reason I'm unhappy?"

I said: "Because I can't completely be there for you."

"Oh," she said, "Gertrud and the child—no, that's not the real reason."

"It isn't?"

"No."

"So what is?" I asked.

She walked next to me, slowly, very calm and composed; I was a little startled at how much strength of spirit, calm, and simplicity she had in her. Then, as I lightly held her arm, she went on: "Who are you, really?

I don't know you. I don't know what you're doing."
She rallied and smiled a little. "What kind of person
you are."

I was shocked. I could feel the strong criticism
behind her words. We were standing by the wooden
barrier.

"I'm a bum," I said. "A better sort of vagabond."

"Please, none of that," she countered. "That's not
what I'm talking about."

"If I were completely free, and I asked you whether
we should stay together, you'd say no."

"No," she said, "I'd say yes—but I'd know what I was
getting myself into."

It all sounded so simple, so unaffected. Again I was
deeply moved. A note sounding, like at the start of our
friendship. A deep bliss. Deep, genuine warmth, her naturalness intact! I was amazed, and very happy. I hadn't
expected that this little person would have thought and
felt so deeply. What an insane idea—that a small person
wouldn't think things through as deeply and genuinely.

But there it was. I had thought it was a schoolgirl
crush on her side. But it wasn't. It is the love, the suffering, of a young woman. Her dear little face. Her slow,
short steps as she walked beside me in the dark.

At the beginning, she said: "I often wish you'd never
written those poems."

I didn't understand. "Why?"

"Because you have such an advantage over me."

"In what? Unhappiness?"

She only smiled.—

End of the conversation with Mrs. Beer about my poems. She thought the second half worked too, especially "Come, sleep!" "Woe unto those," "I often think" [Sonnets XXVI, XXXII, XXIV]— Actually, she found something good in every poem. "War and annihilation" [perhaps XXVII], she thought, had a grim ferocity and grandeur that she also finds in Dante, in Michelangelo. She thinks my poems have an epic, classical quality. I was truly amazed.

Suddenly she asked me: Wasn't I proud of these poems? I said no. And it's true, I'm not specifically proud, just boundlessly happy a lot of the time, filled with overwhelming joy. "No, I'm not" I said. "Sometimes I'm a bit ashamed."

She was furious. How could I be ashamed? Unfortunately I didn't find the right thing to say in response, and I stammered something about being anti-bohemian, afraid of being a literary man, etc. But it isn't that. Not my failure either, in terms of social standing. She was furious, and something broke in the bond between us.

Later she said she wanted to think it over some more. I had shown too little self-confidence as a poet. That must have shocked her. It was wrong of me.

What I think about it now is that I actually *am*

ashamed to write such poetry. In German. I know for a fact that, before I emigrated, and since then, too, there is *no one* in Germany writing such poetry at the moment, and I also have to confess that I often catch myself daydreaming about how someday people in Germany will officially honor me for my poetry—and I will decline the honors. Yes, reject them. That would be my greatest triumph: refusing this recognition. There is only one person I would like to hear praise my poems: Thomas Mann. That would be thanks enough for me.—

I'm curious whether I'll get another letter from Mrs. Beer, about this shame. Maybe I'll type up "To a Dreamer" and send it to her?[122] I have to admit that my poems play a great role in my thoughts and dreams about the future. It will take a long time, but they will secure a place for me among the world's poets writing in the German tongue. And, as a paradoxical case, I will no doubt be in a somewhat unique position. What will Politzer have written? Safe in a neutral country.[123] Will that have been good for him? The poems of his I've read before were worthless—derivative. And yet my goal is to be a doctor.—

I can no longer deny my need to write this diary. But the ultimate zeal to get to the truth is often lacking.

122. See note 10, p. 13.
123. Heinz Politzer (1910–78), a German writer who emigrated to Palestine in 1938.

At least I've broken some bad habits. My skin problem is better too.

Read Hanna's poem, spoken from the point of view of a musical instrument. The line *al koste het een snaar die brak* made me shudder in a way surpassing all literature.[124] It is so completely pure and honest—and so moving, because of the cord I have wrapped around her and tied to me. And then, the ultimate surrender in the last line: "Well then, play." A woman's greatness can so often be her restraint, her renunciation, her "smallness," inconspicuousness. I am so sick to death of important women.

**Friday. 17th.** Night. I just realized why I answered so dismissively, with shame, when I was asked wasn't I proud of my poems. I realized that I have been living like an animal, a dumb beast, for a long time now, for years, almost. And during that time, deeply unhappy, I renounced the writing of poems once and for all. And then they came. When I was no longer expecting it. Is that something I can be proud of? Take credit for? God knows I am unbearably vain often enough, but even I can't feel proud of that. My whole life depends on it. Not some possible social success.

124. "Even if it cost a string, which breaks." There is a Dutch poem by Hanna to "H.K." in Arie Bakker's papers (four quatrains, reproduced in the Dutch edition: *Dagboek 1944*, pp. 168–69, n88), but it does not contain the line Keilson quotes here.

Sent "The Dreamer" to Mrs. Beer today. After typing it out. What a strange poem.— Had Gertrud's face constantly before my eyes, her gaze, her slightly flushed face when she doesn't understand something someone is saying and helplessly turns to me. The nobility of her face. My little Barbara continually in my thoughts too. What would Gertrud say about the poems (the sonnets)?—

Long talk with Cora about Bram, Jan, and herself. She is fighting a difficult battle with her own weapons. How magical it is to see a woman live her life while staying out of it, looking on but at the same time right in her core. It was a therapeutic moment. Of a rare kind. I was relaxed, not eager anymore, not fake anymore. Her life, so brutally on the edge of uncertainty and doubt, was so dear to me—this woman thought only well of me and I could give all these good thoughts back to her. In her naïveté, she said that despite the war she was completely happy, like never before. She couldn't worry about anything except the daily worries that everyone has. But other than that, she was very happy in the new friendship she had found for herself.

**Monday. 11/20.** The light is out. When it comes back on, we'll be free!— This is the night Gertrud dreamed of. It can't last much longer now!

One of the gramophone records we listened to last night was Lou Bandy: *"En ik rij la zo gezellig / op mijn ezeltje door het warme zand / en ik voel mij zo gelukkig / op mijn ezeltje aan het Scheveningsche strand.*"[125] And in Bandy's voice too. There is not a single song I can think of that better captures the mentality of the average Dutchman. The whole world can go to hell as long as I can ride my little donkey across the hot sand. Ta-da!! Can a nation of such people make history? Is it ready and destined to play a role on the world stage? Or any stage? Hooray for what's "nice" and "cozy"![126] *Mijn ezeltje*, my little donkeykin . . .

Wrote more poems. I thought it was done, but apparently a new source has opened up. Including a "Gas!" poem [XXXVII] that seems to me not entirely a failure. Except for the last line—there I have to listen better for how it needs to be. And then the poem "When lordly reason" [XXXVIII]—a poem I'm very excited about.

**Tuesday. 21st.** The Reason poem is finished. I've never spent such a long and concentrated time on any other poem, it seems to me at least—or have I, and just

125. Lou Bandy, Dutch cabarettist and popular singer, 1890–1959: "And I ride so nice and comfy / on my little donkey across the hot sand, / and I feel so nice and happy / on my little donkey on the Scheveningen beach."

126. Keilson uses the typical Dutch adjectives *leuk* and *gezellig*, often called untranslatable, for these absolutely typical Dutch qualities or values.

forgotten? But I can feel a sense of relief too. I'm already on the next one's trail.

Today walked around Delft, in glorious weather. The whole town was on its feet, the trams from The Hague went by filled with arrested men. The conductors stood in front, on the front platforms, weeping, steering. Four English fighter planes circled overhead; there'd been a nice brisk concert in the morning.

Talked to Dr. Kok, head of the field hospital,[127] with whom I'd love to work when it gets to that point. "I have a huge number of poor patients," he said—and I was ashamed. Not only because of the vouchers. It rang so true when he said it. Like a real doctor. Compared to him I again felt like a schlemiel. Thirty-five years old and *still* not a doctor. Versifying my way through the world, singing, exhilarated, full of big ideas—a schlemiel. With wife and child, and a lover. Why was it, actually, that Gertrud always screamed at me and kept track of everything she'd done for me? So I'd turn into a schlemiel like this. She doesn't understand herself. But why couldn't she keep quiet about it. Well, a person is always most ungrateful where he feels in somebody's debt.

Which makes me realize I'm getting old. Men up to age forty are being rounded up, and I'm only five years below the cutoff. Just five. I wished it was at least ten. I

127. See note 118, p. 117.

couldn't understand it: that I was the same person who had walked around in the Charité, and been in Sweden, and in Caputh, with Eva La. Recently I've been dreaming about Freienwalde constantly.[128] I was always so moved when my father used to tell me he had dreamed about something. Now I'm dreaming about Freienwalde.— I would love to walk down those streets. Everything must look completely different now.— And what have I become. What has become of me. A few poems I'm proud of. Is that what's known as giving one's life for the cause? For a few poems. Yes, I'm ashamed, of writing poems. If everything were different, I could have lived naturally. I'm almost bursting with my thoughts. I wonder if one of the doctors I talk to here has noticed. That I actually don't know anything, have no experience at all. Just a bungler.— Only with my little student Bram, Cora's son,

128. Charité, a famous hospital in Berlin; Caputh, a Jewish boarding school where Keilson had taught gym and music. Eva Landauer: a social worker at a day care center, a year older than Keilson, whom he knew in his early twenties. He recalled in a 2009 interview: "Eva played a great role in my life, she was my first inti mate girlfriend. Until one day when she asked my permission to visit an old boyfriend—a Jewish lawyer from Sils Maria that she had known before. I consented, and when she came back it was over. I couldn't stand her having another man besides me" (*Neue Rundschau*, Hans Keilson special issue 120:4 [2009]: 18). Freienwalde, later renamed Bad Freienwalde: the town where Keilson was born and grew up, east of Berlin on the border with Poland.

have I had a little success. That is my field—that's what I can do.

Saw a baby sleeping in its carriage and thought of my little Barbara. Almost had to run out to cry when I wrote that. Everyone was sitting at the table. Shame. What does the future hold. I've actually never felt this entangled. And Gertrud, with whom I'm constantly fighting this secret fight, will have to make up for it somehow. If she agrees that we should separate—amicably separate. Because I can't bring my tensions into our life without it wearing her and the child out.

It's impossible to feel your own age. Someone else who saw me would say: Yes, he's grown older too. Like that doctor in Utrecht: "You do look a bit haggard." And I myself have the feeling of looking at my life only as if through a veil. I know that, but I can't bring the two things into harmony. Just cannot rhyme them. Someday I'll be sixty and I still won't have grasped how it's possible I've grown old. I understand my father better now. If only I knew whether they were still alive. Today, sitting at Arie and Eva's with the two old people, I couldn't help thinking of my own parents, why couldn't they be sitting with us too?

Read in *Crime & Punishment*: Bear up under the suffering, the consequences of your actions. That is justice! Very true—and what a slap in the face to Christianity. Christ suffered the justice of his actions himself.

People who want to love their enemies and crown

them with roses don't understand a thing about what it means to be just to your enemies. Endure like a man what you have to endure, suffer the consequences of your actions, and don't try to spare other people the consequences of theirs. That's the thing! The Christians want to be so just that they save their enemies from the task of being just. And that is impudent vanity. Nothing but.

The razzias are coming here tonight!

**Saturday. 11/25.**    Finished *Crime and Punishment*. The stifling, fantastic air of this exaggerated overexcited air. Then Shestov's essay on Dostoyevsky.[129] Astounding, again and again. [*Illegible*]— the belief that has never worked, that rests on no external authority, that is impossible to grasp. And that still lives on. But not in the law of noncontradiction, which I often used to think was the deepest creation of human thought. Luckily I'm over that. On closer examination, the God of the Old Testament, before whom one trembles, quakes, screams, and hides, is actually a wonderfully perfect personification or representation of the ungraspable. And Judaism— this absurd mix of a vision of God, the truth, and the making of countless laws to destroy that truth. These

129. Lev Shestov (1866–1938), born Jehuda Leib Schwarzmann, whose name Keilson writes in Dutch transliteration (Sjestov, not Schestow), so the essay in question is probably a Dutch translation, presumably from *Crisis of Certainties* (1934). The slight garbling of the sentence repeating "air" is in the original.

laws: given by God. Moses created a people and brought the lie into the world. Thanks to this lie, his people is immortal. His pretence keeps it going. Not his laws. Orthodoxy as the expression of those condemned by God! Orthodoxy as the expression of dependence on feeling an experience of God, but there is fear between the two, a magic invocation through laws and formulas to bring the devil down off one's neck.[130] Psychology to get psychology off one's neck. Free us from psychology. And from the lawfulness of the lawless. Dmitri Karamazov says: Beauty is a terrible thing. It awakens terror.

I come back to my poems, which link love and horror. Those who worship beauty—I sometimes can't escape the thought that they don't understand beauty in the least, they have absolutely no idea what they're worshipping. If they did, they would be terrified and show horror. Look at how beautiful God must be! Dürer's Christ is repulsive, his fear of freedom! The torment of the Jew. He takes his longings and buries them in laws. His return to freedom must be a return from what has been Judaism up to now. But not to Christianity, for God's sake. That would be an even more horrific illusion! To something like early Christianity!

130. Another slip of the pen, merging two phrases that would be natural in German as well as in English: "bring the devil down on one's neck" and "keep the devil off of one's neck."

Gertrud read Spinoza very well, she discovered his burning heart.

I didn't mean "early Christianity," I meant "early Judaism." But there's no difference anymore once you get back to the original "early." The stupidity of people who convert Jews.

Hitler, too, he didn't give the Germans freedom, only authority. The great hater of mankind, the greatest nihilist of the West, devouring his own people!

I always make the same mistake—Dostoyevsky did too—of attributing the other side's truths to earthly things, to social or political facts or institutions. When it's obvious that doing that produces only nonsense and a mess of political mysticism. I was never as honest as I was in my talk with Evert, which he broke off because it didn't satisfy him. There are no norms you can follow in constructing a society. Universal laws—where do they come from, what gives them authority? Reason, logic? It's enough to drive you to despair! But God is not outside of history either! That is a lie, the old fable of the two parallel lines that never intersect. A God outside of history doesn't make God any better or history any worse. Whenever you write or talk about political things, you have to be careful neither to bring the irrational element in nor to leave it out. The art of interpretation. It's not only history that's struggling with this problem. It is much worse in psychology. Surgery, now that's healthy! The little man here, Verschuyl, he's a healer.[131]

I read, in Gautier's introduction to Baudelaire, that Baudelaire despised poetry that lacked self-awareness. So what about Hölderlin, the Orphic poet! It seems to me that I made a very conscious effort, especially in the sonnets, not only to sing but also to give a definite [*word missing*]: Love and horror![132] To bring work into the poetic art. Well, if hard work makes for good poems then I have nothing to worry about. Surely Baudelaire is right—even if he ignores the Orphic aspect, the blind singer. And there are poets like that too. Their labor is subterranean, and accomplished once they have released a poem into the world. To tinker and fiddle around there would be a sin of the intellect against the soul.

**Wednesday. 11/29.**   Very depressed, for many reasons. No news from Gertrud for a long time. Tonight a phone call, news via Cas[133] that Gertrud has bronchitis. But is out of the house again.

131. From the Dutch *heelmeester*, "wound doctor," Keilson writes "*Heilmeister*," a rare German word for doctor (used especially in western territories near the Netherlands) but here probably a Dutchism, or possibly invoking the grander overtones of *Heil* and *Meister*: something like "master healer."
132. See Sonnet XVII.
133. Cas Emmer (1909–2005), Keilson's oldest Dutch friend and his personal physician for decades after the war. Emmer's

With Hanna. Very upsetting. And unpleasant. She asked me why I don't change my passport to make it say 40.[134] "That would never work," I said, "you could tell by looking at me." Convinced that I still looked 20. Where do I get this childish belief from?

"What?" she says. "Everyone says you could easily pass for forty." Startling me. It's not my vanity. No, it's death—so close, so close. That doctor in Utrecht also told me: You look haggard. It's death, nothing else.

Later, was it out of revenge that I was so unaffectionate with the girl? She brings out everything in me, the best and the cruelest. I couldn't stay with her forever.

In this shattered mood, sitting next to her, the first line of a poem came to me. "Immortality?" [Sonnet XLI]— It's as though I provoke myself to these poems, stimulate myself. Bring the fire down from Heaven! Not wait for it to come down on its own. The same as what I read in Baudelaire.

Hanna also told me she feels the mood in the house getting worse, especially about food.[135] Everyone stares

---

circle of friends included Jan Thomassen, Rudi Buys, and the poet Jef Last (see note 162, p. 167).

134. Because of the age limit for conscription to labor service in Germany. This was apparently done, probably with Arie Bakker's help, since Keilson's ID card bore a birthdate of November 10, 1904 (see photo insert).

135. One consequence of the failure of Operation Market Garden (see note 63, p. 67) was the Dutch famine known as the

at one another's plate, no one talks about anything but food. What power hunger has.

She was charming again—but she's not a girl anymore. Still, very attractive. When I was leaving, she cried out, in total despair and complete [*word missing*]: "It can't go on like this forever, that you always just leave!" I don't know what she was imagining. It's disgusting to admit it, but I have to confess that I was delighted by her [*illegible*]tion. This is the cruelest role I can play. It almost kills me—that everything good finds it way into the poem and everything satanic into my human relations . . . I'm a stranger to my own heart sometimes.

I feel the conflict more and more—how am I supposed to become a doctor and go to school while simultaneously doing literary work, without going to the dogs. Ecstasy, ecstasy, wine or love! It's seems almost impossible. I remember what Jan Thomassen said when we were still friends: "We all think you'll eventually give up your medical career and write full-time, if economic

---

Hunger Winter. The Dutch government in London had incited Dutch railway workers to go on strike to help the Allied attack, and in revenge Germany cut off food and fuel shipments to the heavily populated western Netherlands. The blockade was partially lifted in early November, but by then an especially cold and harsh winter had set in, with the canals freezing over and barge traffic becoming impossible. The famine would last until the liberation in May 1945, with some twenty thousand Dutch starving to death.

necessities don't make the decision for you." I wonder if they're right. At the time I thought they were wrong, that a medical career meant more to me than just money. It's that too. But at the same time a huge obstacle!—

Writing here in this surrogate diary frees me somewhat. I can see more clearly: myself, Gertrud, Hanna. But actually it's all just me—the entanglements that arise from my own nature and get projected externally. And the bad choices I make about my environment. I spend time with too many people who make me angry. Including the one who's closest to me most of the time, Gertrud. Apparently my choice of love object contains this element of restlessness too. My restlessness drives me. More than I thought. I used to consider myself bourgeois. Now I see how little of that I have in me. Tonio Kröger, more and more . . . only jumpier!

A lot of time in the hospital, watching various operations. I've learned a lot. Also seen narcotics from up close. Actually better than ever before. Laughing gas too!

**Thursday [11/30].**   I can't help it, Baudelaire's conception of art compels respect only for how serious and honest it is. Not because of what it says. Yes, I too believe that a good poem can only be written from the pleasure of writing a good poem. No attention paid to morality, truth, what have you. But where does the content come from? Baudelaire can't mean to claim that it doesn't matter. He of all people can't. Verlaine might have—the mere singer. But Baudelaire? The moralist.

The truth is, I think Baudelaire was playing hide-and-seek, with us or with himself. The content mattered very much to him, but passing judgment on it didn't. He had a poetic personality so it was in poems that he expressed what he had to say. This led him to discover the "underworld": he was so obsessed, so wrapped up in his topic, in his discovery of this topic, that he didn't even realize how much the discovery meant to him. That's how he could act as though all he cared about was art. This is partly true, though it's even more true for music. Baudelaire's conception applied to music would be almost totally irrefutable. Music actually is the mirroring of the irrational, *in optima forma*. But words have another, symbolic significance. A word is attached to its content, and verbal content is different from sound content. Verbal content remains linked to what the word emerges from; giving meaning to the sound presupposes, i.e. includes, a mental process, which can stand on its own and thus be considered in isolation. The result is an act that can be labeled intellectualism. But at the same moment, while the mental process is trying to represent for itself a lived and still living life, the circle gets bigger. Here a leap occurs, into a realm that cannot be sufficiently covered with the term "the beautiful." There's more to it. For Baudelaire too.

Gertrud and Barbara

Hanna Sanders,
probably soon
after the war

Hans Keilson, 1937
passport photo

Hans Keilson, passport photo
as Dr. van der Linden

Suus and Leo
Rientsma

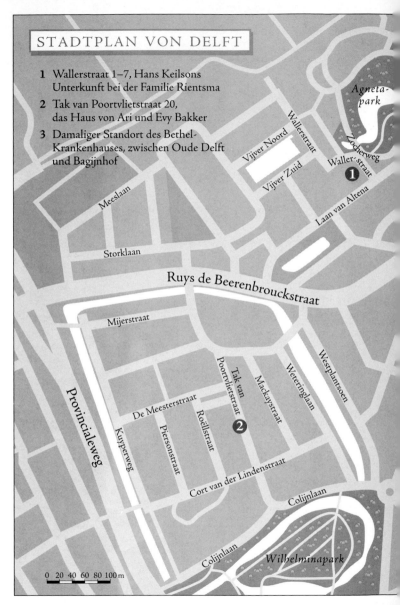

# STADTPLAN VON DELFT

1 Wallerstraat 1–7, Hans Keilsons
Unterkunft bei der Familie Rientsma

2 Tak van Poortvlietstraat 20,
das Haus von Ari und Evy Bakker

3 Damaliger Standort des Bethel-
Krankenhauses, zwischen Oude Delft
und Bagijnhof

*Agneta-park*

Vijver Noord

Wallerstraat

Zocherweg

Waller-straat

❶

Vijver Zuid

Meeslaan

Laan van Altena

Storklaan

Ruys de Beerenbrouckstraat

Mijerstraat

Provincialeweg

Westplantsoen

Weteringlaan

Mackaystraat

Tak van Poortvlietstraat

Mijerstraat

De Meesterstraat

Roëllstraat

❷

Kuyperweg

Piersonstraat

Cort van der Lindenstraat

Colijnlaan

Colijnlaan

*Wilhelminapark*

0  20 40 60 80 100 m

**MAP OF DELFT**

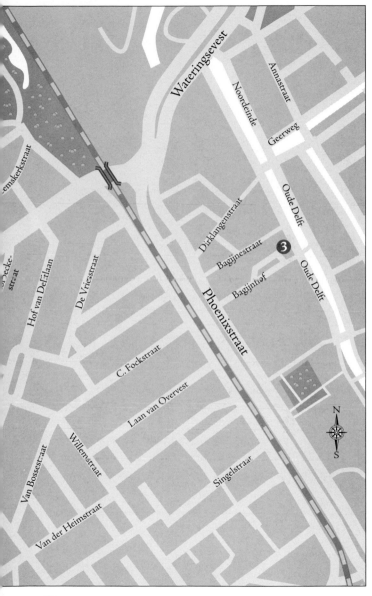

① **Wallerstraat 1–7: Hans Keilson's lodging at the Rientsmas'**
② **Tak van Poortvlietstraat 20, where Hanna Sanders lived with the Bakkers** ③ **Bethel Hospital**

Hanna Sanders and Evy Bakker

ID for "Johannes Gerrit van der Linden" (Hans Keilson); note birth date was changed from 1909 to 1904 so that he would be over forty in December 1944

G 41   № 330891

van der Linden--

Johannes Gerrit--

10 November 1904
Semarang
Nederlandsch Indië

Evy and Arie Bakker, March 1943

When he had to replace Racine's language with a new one because the old one was no longer applicable, no longer sufficient, in that same movement he went a step farther, or deeper, into the life of his time and himself. At the very least, he should have understood clearly that his new mastery of language was not only a matter of aesthetics, but something more. And that the word, as a symbol, comes trailing another realm behind it; it awakens and excites something in the reader that a purely aesthetic or artistic viewpoint would only violently shut down again after the fact.

Many of his poems are closed off for me. And the odd thing is: nowadays Baudelaire's intellectual importance is at least as recognized as his purely poetic importance. He must be turning over in his grave. But he, and his poems too, have more to do with truth than he might like. What he found were, to some extent, analytic truths. Amazing, actually. Baudelaire, Nietzsche, Dostoyevsky. Nietzsche got so much farther. Baudelaire was still too caught up in idealistic philosophy and its conceptual world to penetrate through it to the truth of a life—a truth that no longer has anything to do with the intellect, but only with the parasympathetic nervous system. That Baudelaire wrote his poems with more than just his pencil or quill—who needs proof of that. And in so doing he refuted himself. Better than anyone else could have. *La poésie n'a pas d'autre but qu'elle même*.[136] But to reach that goal, a life is necessary. Didn't God demand from Abraham nothing but a life? In short: Poetry has no goal, it has only sources—all of which come, flow, from life and into life. It is self-presentation: an unending path from nothingness to nothingness. Art for art's sake is as much a prejudice as the prejudices of Romanticism or morality, the truth that it's denying.

**Sunday. 12/3.**   The mood improved so much after a good meal. Leo came home with a goose.[137] Even so, I felt terrible, violent envy over how it was divided up, a feeling I struggled against in vain. Apparently they felt the same way, because the next day it was better. How a person's mood depends on his stomach. On new stimulation.

Started a poem, stopped after the first 8 lines and started two more poems that I finished. Including the "Immortal Poem" that I love [Sonnet XLII]. Worked exceptionally hard on it. Still more work to do.

Word comes that there is still bread for two weeks. Then what? I get anxious and scared thinking of Gertrud

---

136. "Poetry has no aim but itself": Baudelaire's credo, repeated in several essays.
137. A near-miracle during the Hunger Winter, and one that the Rientsma daughters would remember their whole lives.

and the child. Will worse come to worst? Gertrud's dream come true?

Night already. No more light.

Closer connection with Cora. She looks at me so expectantly, as though asking something from me. A happy friendship. She is often very depressed.—

I have watched a lot of surgeries recently and that strengthens my resolve to do my utmost to become a doctor, or stay a doctor. Will I find a way? And then what. And where? It will all still be so hard. For now, I live happily in my poems.—

Worried about Gertrud's health. Annemarie's calm voice on the phone.[138] Is it her lungs? *Poète maudit.* I have the life I've so often asked for. And now I'm complaining? Yes—I was asking for these complaints too, they're part of it.

Constantly think about my youth in Freienwalde. I could spend hours describing it. Why didn't I go to South America with Happ?[139] I could have learned a lot. And been at a safe distance. Why do I constantly criticize

138. Annemarie Pfeiffer (b. 1922), Gertrud's daughter from her first marriage.

139. Dr. Happ was the Keilson family doctor in Bad Freienwalde, whom Keilson remembered fondly. Keilson visited him in Israel in 1969 and left the following unpublished description: "His waiting room was full of Arab patients, some of them in bedouin clothing. He spoke to them in a language I understood absolutely

and correct myself in so many things, retouching my life all over, now that I am set and have basically figured out who I am, as an artist. It's strange how I recoil from writing the word "artist." But it's all about the rewriting. I calculate, correct, readjust, change this and that, re-touch my life, and in so doing am more sharply defined than ever. Maybe that's why I do it. Maybe it's the feel-ing of expressing myself, of gradually emptying myself out into the poems, that makes me reach back into the earlier stages of my life, when I was desperate to do cre-ative work. The feeling of inwardly being raised up into a state of bliss still washes over me like giant waves, the same as when I was a boy, in front of my father's door at 7 a.m. on the street with the sun rising above it. I felt alive. Soon, when I'm back at home with wife and child, I'll be dead. And yet I love them. Gertrud has helped me this far, she will continue to help me.

[*The following entry is written in pencil.*]
**Saturday. 12/9/44.**   The children think I've climbed out the window. Maybe not Lieske, she's older and under-stands more. I've been up for 1½ hours, sitting in Leo's cluttered room. An indescribable mess. Typewriter, countless little lamp batteries, boxes of tiny lightbulbs,

---

nothing of, but the way he was with them—calm, friendly, patient—was exactly the same as when he was seeing patients in Freienwalde."

newspapers, screws, wire, dust, soldering irons. German police patrolling on the street and in the park. Short bursts of gunfire. One time I heard—at least I think I heard—screams right after the shots. Manhunt in Delft. Suus woke me up at 4:45, and at the same time I heard the doorbell ringing like crazy. We've been ready for this signal for days, for weeks. Now it's here, and even so, it's a little eerie—constant gunshots, now closer, now farther off . . . Suus helped me crawl through the closet. The slow tread of military boots on the sidewalk out the window. The policeman is carrying his rifle diagonally across his chest now. Half an hour ago I saw him on Laan van Altena taking aim at a nurse who wasn't going fast enough. *Wacht even, alsjeblieft*, she screamed as loud as she could, *alsjeblieft*.[140] The good Dutch people—they just can't get it through their heads how it is. Thank God. This surplus of horrors exceeds their plodding imaginative abilities.— The men who report for work duty are promised good treatment, rations, and tobacco. Families staying behind will be taken care of. What this care will consist of is not said, unfortunately. Voices— on the street? Or from the neighbors? I peer through the tulle curtains. Nothing outside. It is cold and bright. The Oude Kerk and Nieuwe Kerk spires poke up over the gabled roofs into a yellow-red strip of sky with a thick blue-black clump of cloud floating above it. A light

140. "Wait, wait, please! . . . Please!"

wind blows the cloud banks slowly over the bare tree-tops in the park to the south. When the sliding doors in the house or the neighbors' are slid open—Mr. van Oyen[141] has the voice of a kraut, despite his predilection for English literature. But the soldiers always speak in groups; I won't be fooled again. I imagine they're Austrians, incidentally.— The sound of the sliding doors makes you think a V-2 is going up. Then, when the noise suddenly stops, you think that it's peaked and is falling back down to earth. The span of time from when the noise stops to the explosion that follows—6 seconds, 10 seconds—is the interval Death leaves you to prepare for him. (Don't look out the window, Corrie, they're shooting into the houses too.) Afterward, after the explosion, the building still shaking, first a deep sigh of relief that it didn't land here. And immediately after that, conscience: The poor people who *were* where it came down. That's how people are. Sin and conscience. Both seem to be metaphysical instincts. The room is cold. A train whistle blows. You can hear it starting up. Only two engines, facing each other, moderate speed. It's a special event after two months of railway strike, like when the mail arrives in a remote mountain village isolated from life elsewhere.—

Whoever disobeys the conscription order will be

141. The van Oyens, friends of the van der Leks, lived on the upper floor of Wallerstraat 5 after being evacuated from The Hague.

punished. I don't seem to have thought for a second about whether to report. It would be what people call insane, to stay in hiding for a year and a half and then, right before the end of the war, to voluntarily put myself in their hands. Up to now I've been "underground" but free to move around on the street like a normal person. Now I'll have to truly disappear. Stay in the house.— Again, the wild temptation to do the opposite comes over me. To report for duty after all, try to become a doctor. In Germany. That's the quickest path to the job. The Dutch housewives are beating their rugs in front of their doors, making a banging noise. Every sound nowadays is part of the soundscape of the war. You can hear in this rug-beating protest, pride, all the rebelliousness a proud population is capable of. Only Hanneke, our neighbors' eight-year-old little girl, starts practicing her finger exercises on the piano.[142] They don't have anything to do with any of this. Disobedience is one of the best and most valuable qualities I know. I mean refusing to follow the prescribed, sensible course of events, refusing to behave properly, the way *one* expects you to behave. This "one" is the devil of civilization. The great tempter, urging you to leave everything else untried, untested. The Germans don't have much of it—for them, subordination and obedience is the Lord's Prayer, unfortunately the God they pray to is stupidity, and the church where

142. The van Oyens' daughter.

they pray to this God is the Party. Herr Himmler its pope! What would it be like, if I did it after all? And lost my life in the process. I knew the Germans so well when I left. Back then they were so intoxicated with victory, and I was so downcast. To see them again now—after all they've been through—that would be the most crushing revenge I can imagine: to live among them incognito and read in their faces the downward path they're on. They would have no idea that there was a scout in their midst, a spy—gunshots, gunshots, left-hand piano from Hanneke—to whom they were mercilessly, unguardedly revealing their deepest secrets. That would be the greatest pleasure imaginable. (It is in fact an Austrian. I heard him talking in front of the window with a neighbor; she wanted some sort of information from him. He was apparently perfectly willing to give it. He laughed at the end and kept his hands in his pockets. Strange, that someone who carries a rifle and aims it at a nurse laughs. Apparently our thoughts about these German police, who also carried out the razzias for Jews in Amsterdam, have taken on such forms that we can now only picture them as monstrous demons. Clinging to these bogeyman superstitions doesn't speak well of us. Since they have no connection with the truth. Even the executioners in the concentration camps are not always like that. Sometimes, when they're with a lady, they too can melt away into something that has nothing to do with camps and executioners. And if we happened to meet such a man in private life, where that side of his nature is turned toward us, we would suddenly be inclined to stop believing in the other side. "He's not as bad as all that!" If our mental picture of the left side is wrong, we decide that the right side must be misrepresented too. Beware of German policemen who are "also" human beings! They are the best at doing their duty, because, when the time comes, they do their job faithfully and well. They are the gentleman criminals.— It's getting boring here, nothing's happening. Less gunfire. More women turning up on the streets, to get bread. It's strange how the appearance of a woman in the chaos and horror adds a note that seems to belong. Of insubordination, of sedition, maybe that's it. Prepared to endure, to accept, and along with that the will to resist. Women could prevent wars—but that would mean destroying the lives that are built on the suppression of rebellion. The soldier—technical, organized, in uniform—and the woman—spontaneous, chaotic joy and disgust. The soldier smiles; he is won over. A couple of women on the street, going to get bread, grumbling, cursing—but they are getting bread, because even going to get bread is not just an everyday task—the everyday is, in extraordinary times, as sublime, incomprehensible, and incredible as the extraordinary. Hanneke, playing her scales while there's shooting on the street outside. The everyday moves us, just as terror does. The policeman has stopped shouting. He paces up and down the street with his hands buried deep in his coat pockets, rifle diagonally over his shoulder with the barrel pointing at the ground. He seems to have calmed down. His fear has faded. I wonder what he's like in private life. Women and girls with milk canisters. They shout across the street. It won't be much longer now, then they'll bring the policeman a cup of tea. They walk so defiantly, with their brightly colored canisters. And the cup of tea, the soldier mustn't imagine it means anything, it is no proof of friendship, no more than if they slept with him. It's an act of defiance. Their way of fighting, their declaration of war. The pond in the park, with its sinuous shape, lies bleak and bare. The winter trees have locked life up inside them. They're waiting, too; the leaves fell in autumn. They can see from the people, and even more from the birds sitting few and far between on their wet trunks and branches, that it's winter.

I've started reading Kafka, *The Trial*! The purity, the pronouncement . . . I'm amazed to realize that in my *The Sacrifice*[143] I am

[*breaks off*]

They came. I saw them form groups in front of the park gate and march into the park. I disappeared into my hiding place inside the rear outer wall of the attic where the two girls sleep. I felt very calm, not in the least like I

143. A novel in progress.

was in a tense situation. Everyone stayed calm, especially Leo. I heard muffled voices downstairs, doors slamming. I thought I could hear voices from down the courtyard too. After all, I was inside the rear wall of the building. After a while, it all started to seem rather comic to me in a way, and so, to at least inject a little suspense and inner action into what was happening, I tried thinking about Gertrud and Barbara. But the only thing that came to me was what I would say to Gertrud later when she asked me about what I'd been through. "I hid." That was it, really. After a while I heard muffled steps coming closer. I was wearing my thick winter coat, scarf, gloves, and hat. My head was lying on soft pillows, on a mattress. Someone slid open the wooden door—the entrance to my hiding place—and just then I heard Leo speaking, uninterruptedly, as though talking to someone. I had no idea who. I understood this: "Yes, and we have another hiding place here, look," and he slid the wood aside. The thought raced through my head for a tiny millisecond, no more: "What's *this*?" But nothing more. Suddenly someone grabbed me by the leg. "I'm coming on my own," I said, in the same tone of voice. "You've promised good treatment and rations, right?" And I forced myself to come out. Leo stood there laughing. It was over. They had gone into the rabbit hutch and had a nice little talk. "Good," the soldiers had said before leaving. (A V-2, two booms, it's aiming right at us, I hear it, the sound cuts out, the impact is coming any second, it's raining, pouring, hailing, I wake up.)[144] They were Austrians. I went downstairs to Leo's room. A soldier was standing in the middle of a lawn outside, and he fired a shot. Then he walked a few steps and picked up something from the ground. He had shot a bird. He knocked the bird against a wooden fence. After a while, footsteps came from the park area in back. Six young men, each carrying a potato sack tied shut on his back, turning slowly sullenly sluggishly onto the park path, guarded by three policemen. A sad procession. They were mostly young guys, under thirty, bareheaded. They wore blue overalls under their coats. Bareheaded. They held their heads up high in an unusual way, not as though with pride but the way people do when, completely unwillingly, they have submitted to a stronger will without offering resistance. Those who do offer resistance and are defeated lower their heads in shame at their weakness—Corrie, standing next to us, burst into tears. She said a curse word, a German curse word, as though even a Dutch *word* would be too good for them. She must be remembering the razzias for Jews in Amsterdam, where she lost two children. Only now, as I calmly watched others fall into the trap, did it start to dawn on me how much danger I had been in and had

144. Leo's practical joke about betraying Keilson was apparently a kind of dream sequence; Leo was known for his jokes.

just escaped. But even this new awareness left me more or less unmoved. I felt mild surprise, since I would have thought I'd have been more nervous, with my excitable nature. I don't want to lose myself in digressions here about why I was less nervous than I might have been. Maybe it's enough to say that I've achieved a greater distance from my own personal experiences, compared to before. A policeman went to our next-door neighbor on the right, and I disappeared up into the hiding place again. I nestled into my coat and lay outstretched, unmoving, a little clammy in the dim, narrow hiding place, and dozed off. This time it took longer before Corrie came and let me out.

Bram came to me on his own and told me about his way of working. About the deep dissatisfaction he felt, and more. He ended by asking me to work with him more. He wanted more tasks.— A small victory for me, also in assessing their Watering's reports. He came on his own, and he himself pointed out the path he should follow. That is how a therapist should always work—so that the children come when they want and take what they need. Oh, Wilm Gallwitz, I first learned this from you—and Ernst Burkhart, even more from you.[145] Both

145. Wilhelm (Wilm) Gallwitz (1900–81) was an actor at the Bad Freienwalde summer theater in the late twenties; in an unpublished fragment, Keilson describes "a tall, thin, good-looking man, playing the lover [i.e., lover characters in plays]. Another boy my age and I used to take walks with him in the woods that

of you are so present in my work. Are you still alive, or did the English bombs get you?

[*End of the penciled entry*]

**Tuesday XII.12.** A hard, unfriendly day,[146] filled with Suus's failed attempts to be nice and Leo's honest friendship, which isn't enough to warm my spirits. What an utter lack of warmth and spontaneous kindness. I never would have thought I'd feel the lack this strongly. Accustomed as I am to Gertrud's warmth. Felt miserable. Cora came, her children too, that was a bright spot. One more illusion gone! I thought that if I really was part of their home the way they say I am, they would have prepared something. I thought that the time I spent with the children would have counted for a little bit more. I'm sure this isn't their intention, it's just—like everything—a little human indifference, interpersonally. By which I don't mean to say: indifference as such.

---

could easily have been slightly seductive. Later I met him again in Berlin, and still later in Göttingen. He had given up his acting career, was married, and was editor of a large regional newspaper. The force of attraction he had exerted on me, as an actor and a person, had disappeared. But he was still the same friendly person as before, and still liked me."

Ernst Burkhart was a district assessor who introduced Keilson to Thomas Mann's "Tonio Kröger" (see note 111, p. 113). He is fictionalized as Dr. Köster in Keilson's autobiographical first novel, *Life Goes On* (pp. 116ff.).

146. Keilson's thirty-fifth birthday.

Not in the mood to brood on big things. I hope that by doing all this I'll save my life. That's all. If it gets the job done, it's good.

Started reading Shakespeare's sonnets. Together with Stefan George's translations. They are both so extraordinary that I am almost reeling. What poetry! Particularized down to the smallest detail, every feeling brought to a rare clarity and transparency, poetically complete in every way. Not just feeling, but also, powerfully: intellect. But they don't make me feel despair about my own sonnets in comparison. I don't measure mine against them. I am absolutely certain: Everyone has to follow his own little path! And I mine. What will last in the poems—I almost don't care about that anymore. And Hanna is all but forgotten. A delicious aftertaste, and a danger to my conscience, which is often despairing anyway. But I've become rough and brutal, so "I celebrate life in the poem." It's as though what I was afraid of for so long has disappeared. As for life with Gertrud and the child, I fear the worst. My conscience doesn't stop me from taking things from people, letting myself have my way with what's theirs. Pang of conscience? One more wrinkle carved into my face? A deep confirmation of being, pushing up from the slime and nothingness. No illusions—hard on both sides. Risks are the whetstone of character. So love your whetstone.

Conversations in my mind with Gertrud. Fights, wrestling. Alternating with fears that she's sick. Her lungs. That would mean an end to our life together. A desperate end. Not to my love for her, which would no doubt be reinvigorated by her illness. *Voilà, est un homme!* How can a thirty-five-year-old man have such doubts? Everything dissolves into nothing. Becomes smoke, fog, Christian Hell—I understand the founders of religions, these heroes of fear. And smart alecks.

This year I worked a lot and wrote a lot. And am not done yet. Kafka reinforces my plan to continue in this concentrated way, maybe without giving up a medical career, doing both. And the other thing is life. Life. But normal life—no tension, no excitement. If I can. But Tolstoy lived like a dog too. Gertrud, my scourge!

Kafka's literary mode seems to me the only possible way to write today. A concentration, a working through of everything, bordering on the miraculous. The novel *The Trial*, a fragment like so many great works of art, transparently works out its main idea. Original sin, the question of the innocent person's culpability. The trial that never results in acquittal, only apparent acquittal, or else abduction. And the thorn in the soul that he shows us—this unavoidable[147] pushing to see the trial

147. In German *unaufwendbar*, which means "unspendable" (literally, something you can't use), but is here probably a slip of the pen blending *unabwendbar* (inescapable, something you can't turn away from) and *unaufhaltsam* (unstoppable).

through to the end. Maybe it's merely a drive, a compulsion, to undergo his trial. The urge for self-justification in someone who feels himself to be innocent. This paradox. This having to do something in order to show that you haven't done anything wrong. And yet, the trial is often the only way to come into contact with the higher authorities, the judges of the highest court. Even the men who take him away at the end have this connection—an abducting connection to the higher authorities. You'd have to say that this tactic of abduction is desirable, since it keeps the thorn in. It's actually *la condition humaine*. Keeping the thorn in. And not despairing. What happens to K. in the end? His trial never comes to an end. What does that mean for him. Does that have consequences for his life? Does he shoot himself? Or get married? Or not do anything? Ultimately, the trial has only one meaning, insofar as it has "his" meaning.

Kafka must have been a man absolutely possessed by religion, tortured into a quivering mass by the question of original sin. And then to be able to present it so powerfully. Unfortunately, he hasn't clarified for me what it meant to him in his own life. It meant everything—as far as I know. But I don't know much. It must have influenced his personal decisions, to the very end. It's obvious how he felt about artistic work, literary work. He burned his papers. With a grimness that no self-destructive impulse could match. Strange that these questions can only lead to a dissolution of the self.— And then I think about Gertrud and I'm scared. My love for her is just fear.

It has taken me a long time to feel the question of original sin as a festering wound. The human being is sinful? I, sinful!? Sinful=going against the agreements that decency and loyalty are built on. Well then, decency and loyalty, what does that mean? And on it goes, up to the highest form. And then you're supposed to see that at the moment you lose the idea of sin, the divine with its lordly scale of values recedes. The idea of sin is necessary for us, so as not to fall into the sin of godlessness. Heaven stands or falls with sin. Not religion, though—that has another possible mode of communion, self-reflection, and connecting to a world beyond. How alien to me this whole story of sin is, ultimately. I am a sinful creature? This formulation would only make me laugh, if I wasn't also ready with my grief when I feel something like the terror of love. That's not incompatible with feeling deeply moved, stirred to the depths. But sin? The struggle between different possible pleasures is supposed to be a sin? Humankind driven out of the garden? A beautiful poetic construction, whose traces we can feel all the way down to Freud. But this creature made of dust and eternity is raised up, permitted to live. Lament and praise, terror and love, that's it. Where is there room for sin. How I treat Gertrud—is that sinful behavior? I cannot bow down to a law that would judge and condemn me like this.

**12/14.** That which is written is unalterable, and the opinions about it are often nothing but despair.[148] This sentence, maybe the deepest of all of Kafka's brilliant thoughts, is what struck me most from *The Trial*. Despair. So that is the key to someone who wants very much to believe, of whom belief is demanded, and who nevertheless can no longer find the path to belief. Before it stands the doorkeeper, guarding the law, and the man from the country dies before the doorkeeper's eyes after spending his life waiting there. This stirs something deep inside of me, something I have been running away from in many possible forms for years! Art, too, is just one form of it. Kafka knew that, otherwise his mysterious relationship to his own work would be inexplicable! My creative stagnation, for years, always starting over and never finishing anything, was probably for a related reason. It's meaningless, really. You can't expect salvation from that! You can't expect salvation from art. In other words, art cannot heal.

The relationship to religion—for me it is not being firmly grounded in a solid, stable faith but rather a succession of shamings, conscience, violence, and fear. Kafka brings me—not closer to the Law, but he shows

148. Slightly misquoted from near the end of *The Trial*: words spoken by a priest to Josef K. in a dimly lit church ("That which is written is unalterable, and opinions about it often merely express despair over it"). The priest goes on to tell Josef K. the parable "Before the Law."

me the "Before the Law." The Law, in its innermost core, contains faith, religion. We remain Before the Law. What it has planned for us remains invisible. Did God want to punish humanity with the law? As Pascal and Shestov show. Or not? Well, if this punishing is truly how it is, then the man's behavior before the law is bizarre. His obedience to the doorkeeper. I was waiting with bated breath to see whether he would obey him. I hoped he wouldn't. But what did he do? He stayed there, sitting before the law. He immediately believed what the doorkeeper told him. Of course it was a lie. They wanted to see what he would do when he was denied entrance. And he pulled up a stool and sat there until he died. Unbelievable! How can you just sit on a stool and wait, next to a pointy-nosed doorkeeper. He could have at least taken one step further at some point. Dammit, wasn't he even a tiny bit curious?! Surely it wasn't all about the doorkeeper, or the question of who was free here and who was constrained, but about what the stranger would do with the information he received. Again: It's unbelievable that he would just pull up a stool and stay there and wait. I would have said *Bon jour*, or something. I would have looked for another way in. Or else: "What! A shabby doorkeeper like you wants to keep me out!"? He can kiss my ass! Why not that, Kafka, why not? It *is* enough to make a person despair.

This damn transcendence. Hadn't Kafka heard of Spinoza?—had he already so fundamentally missed that connection in himself. Anyway, he's right. But not the way he wrote it. That only makes you furious at this guy. For heaven's sake, to pull up a stool and just sit there! It's the problem of the negative of revelation: It happened once. One time! And then was lost again. That's wrong— either it never happened (except in the imagination, but that doesn't count), and then it can't be lost, or it did happen, and then too it cannot truly be lost, because nothing is lost, here. Or it could always be found again. The key can always be found again, or made. But this accursed transcendence, which leaves the "making" up to immanence and at the same time despises it. Who says that Kafka, with his attitude, his despair, *didn't* have "the key" to faith. (Don't laugh, Klages!)[149] Who can say whether HE, Franz Kafka—when he says "I don't know, help, I am in despair"—doesn't hold the positive revelation in his hands. *He* doesn't know. He can't. Of course not. He would have to be out of his mind, i.e. in his case out of his vanity and *in* his cold sober reasoning mind!! That's it. But the man from the country stays before the door, the open door, sitting on his stool next to this fool of a doorkeeper— No, we'll never forgive Kafka for that. That the man from the country just sat there.

Incidentally, Kafka himself left. Apparently he knew it himself. Because he was ashamed when he wrote down his own burning untruth!—

149. See note 17, p. 18.

But you never can get to the end of it. I'm stuck right at the beginning of my novel *The Sacrifice*,[150] it needs to find territory of its own to occupy. Willibald wouldn't wait. He would dare to go in, and anyone who tried to block his entry would get a punch in the face. I have to finish this novel. Chapters of it will be practically plagiarism. But that won't stop me! Just get through it. The law is the original sin, the court of judgment through which God manifests himself!

Incidentally, *The Trial*'s ending is impossible. Almost lyrical, with the beautiful death, survived by shame.

Aha. I've just read in an unfinished chapter, "Elsa," that "one should try to bring the instruments of power down upon one's head" to find out what they are. Aha—but it remained unfinished. Very unfinished, in fact. What an honest confession! Kafka didn't want to have anything to do with instruments of power of this kind. Too bad Kafka didn't keep writing here. Dereliction of duty, desertion. Or did he despair of his despair? He did know his Kierkegaard, didn't he? Too bad!

**Thursday. 12/21.**    Something has happened. But what? I wrote the 46th sonnet more for Gertrud than for Hanna. Or you could say: the occasion for the poem has

150. See note 143, p. 148. Willibald, mentioned in the next sentence, is the novel's protagonist.

retreated farther and farther behind the poem. The necessary development for every artistic work. Distancing from the object in life. *L'art pour l'art*.[151] But it's more than this, it is not just an aesthetic problem. It is being pulled into the whole circle of life. But detaching from the girl is probably necessary, and time helps. Has that string inside her broken, which she once wrote that she would accept if it was a solution for her? Her nature speaks to me differently now, more lovingly, even in its unnatural constraint. What I'm left feeling is something like duty. But Gertrud, and the child—I suddenly feel closer to them than ever. They were in danger, and danger has always brought us together. The people here, too, seem gentler than before. Something has happened.

If you push and push you eventually force a way to your center. I work like a mole. But unfortunately, still many mysteries and pitfalls of character. The traitorous, thieving nature I suffer under. And cannot overcome. Nibbling crumbs from the table is something the unfree do. I didn't realize that that's what I was, to such an extent. Deep shame.

Shakespeare's sonnets have both harshness and sweetness. Power and gentleness. Music and shape. Sound and color. And unquestionable proof of an eminent life behind them. It's strange that we don't know who they

151. "Art for art's sake."

were written to. This elevates their mystical significance for us, almost. And gives each individual sonnet an infinite perspective.

Deep admiration for Stefan George too—his language is comparable only to Luther's. You don't know who to admire more, Shakespeare or George.

"And no one will cry Victory!"—this remark is increasingly confirmed.[152] We'll see more in the next few days. Will Churchill fall? His shadow is tilting down to the ground, more and more.

Van Oyen read my "Dreamer." He thought it was very pure and concentrated. I didn't tell him it was mine. Very tempted to.

**22nd.** Last night already I learned what had happened, when Olga came and brought a letter from Gertrud.[153] So resigned, and at the same time so sweet—Gertrud never wrote to me like that before, the way she does now that she's sick. I feel despair, feel horribly guilty. Are my poems truly written with her blood after all? It's shattering to think that my Dadaut

152. Possibly a reference to a Stefan George poem, "The War," written toward the end of World War I: "[T]hey shall not cheer; no triumph will mark the end / only downfalls and destruction inglorious."

153. Olga Gülcher or, probably, her daughter, referred to below as Little Olga; see note 25, p. 29.

is sick, with TB. Why is she so sorely tested? First the child,[154] now this.

What can I do? It's all so hard. And the stupid letters I sometimes wrote her. I remember how she came to me when I was sick at Ommen.[155] I can see her tottering down the lane with her little suitcase in hand. As long as it's not her lungs. In other words, it is her lungs. But maybe not an active infection yet. Then she'd need to rest for months. I'm just frivolously playing games with my life, my wife and child. No, not frivolous: whipped on by a daemon. I want to tear up my poems. But they are the only thing I'll have to stand on when the resurrection comes. My only ticket. There's nothing else! Who is it decreeing all this? Fatality, catastrophe!

Her letter made me cry. And I now know that my heart, which I thought was with Hanna, is actually only with her. These entries are my black procession of witnesses: that I have been shaken to the very roots of my existence by her, the way I am by no one else. But what good is that now. The tests in the hospital are today. I will try to get there by [illegible] or boat or bicycle. But I *have to* see her and talk to her. And the child too, something's wrong with her too. This train

154. Either referring to their son, Tom, born dead in 1940, or perhaps to Barbara's kidney problems, discussed below.
155. See the first entry in the diary. In the summer of 1943, Keilson occasionally left Rekken to work at the Quaker School in Ommen, where Ida ter Haar, Jef Last's wife, worked.

situation[156] is the last straw for Gertrud. The exploding bombs. Is that what remains for her?[157] An illness? Is that the ransom of heaven? Have mercy, permit a little delay before the final reckoning! Does Gertrud actually think I want a separation? I don't have the magical fear I had back then with Ida von S.[158] It's different. *Maudit, maudit.*

Constantly thinking of Gertrud. And I try to picture what her life is like now. All I manage to do is summon up an endless sadness in myself. I see her careworn face, aged, full of grief, bent over the child. I'm tortured by these images. They pursue me without end. Art is shit. Human powerlessness. Just like how Suus loves her dog Pronkie.[159] Without the power to grasp and hold what is always changing. And the silence. The life within limits. Such solitude, such loneliness.

Gertrud's horrifying solitude. If only I could do something.

It is not ugliness or hatred when I write the following: Suus, tonight, "Oh, Hans"—her voice sounding very happy—"I finally found something for you to give."

156. A German munitions train was hit by an English plane on the railway line to Naarden on November 30, with the resulting explosion causing damage to a wide area, including Van Halllaan.

157. The image from the end of "To a Dreamer"; see note 10, p. 13.

158. Unknown.

159. Which suffered from epilepsy.

"Give who?" I ask, even though I know it's for Lieske.
"For Lieske's birthday."

"Oh," I say, and I think: What kind of an idiot are you, can't you see I've been crying?

She goes on: "We're giving her the little purse, so you can give her something that fits inside it, a little mirror, I'll look and see if I have an old compact. An old mirror from a purse of mine."

As God is my witness, that's how she said it. And I see the blushing, embarrassed face of someone I otherwise like, and I think she just doesn't want me to spend any money. And she says so in the only way she possibly can, namely a totally impossible way. What a person, what a woman! You rarely see such a combination of kindheartedness and obliviousness.[160] And yet I owe her so much.

But Cora's warm kindness felt good. Spontaneity, protest—it reminds me of how Gertrud is.

Cas let me down too.[161] No surprise there. Little Olga confirmed it. He's a weakling too. Are his conflicts signs of strength or weakness? And am I any better? I don't know. But I do think I'm a more reliable friend. Less belletristic. Gertrud, so alone. Her lungs are in pain, like the pain she feels from love. As though I'd

160. *Trägheit*—see note 95, p. 92.
161. What this refers to is not known. Cas Emmer and Keilson remained lifelong friends; see note 133, p. 134.

forgotten. I've realized that I'm a Jew again from the blows raining down on us from the other party in the sacred bond. Anyway, it's good that I'm being forced out of my Fake-Happy Period. But too bad for the one who was the object of it. Now we're being brought closer again to all the others in Poland and the concentration camps. As long as the child recovers. There's something wrong with her kidneys. Always thirsty, always has to pee. I can picture it all in my mind, Gertrud crouching by the child sitting on the potty, amazed that there's so much coming out.

When I told Suus about Barbara, the first thing she said was to describe another child whose kidney problems were so bad that the doctor said the child couldn't be saved. Thanks a lot! I said nothing. It really was incredibly encouraging.—

The old God doesn't abandon us, my mother used to say. He hasn't abandoned us. It's true. He has remembered us in the olden way, impossible to misunderstand. Anyone who doubts is quickly disabused of that. Gertrud won't misunderstand it either. And every time, I vow and swear that it will be different this time. That I'll be there for her. And then I run away again. Until the next promise.

But it's strange, for six months now I've known that the war won't simply end for us, with me coming back unscathed to an unscathed family in an unscathed home. I'm almost relieved that it's happened like this. Even though I wasn't scared waiting for it. Instead, in a grim way, a kind of premonition in me has been confirmed. Come closer to being fulfilled. With hellish laughter, heaven has kept the promise it made. You have to be grateful to it, for its constancy. Reliable like nothing else.

Hanna wanted to come over. I asked Evy not to send her, I don't want to upset her. Said Evy should tell her it's not as bad as Corrie made it sound.

Little Olga is very sweet and nice. A little woman. She took good care of me. What will become of her later? Will she and Werner get together? I almost suspected that she is already a woman. But I might be wrong. I wrote to her mother and asked her to continue to help Gertrud. She'll do it. Gertrud absolutely needs fatty food. I don't know if I'll be able to help her. Will I be able to get to her by bicycle? Can I?

Suus observes me secretly and I observe her openly. She doesn't really understand much about life. A very peculiar person. Means well. But no depth. Still, good and useful. A terrible conflict for me.

Cas sent me Jef's poems.[162] A Chinese title: *Tao Ko Tao*.

162. Jef Last (1898–1972), a sinologist, prolific Dutch poet and prose writer, and gay activist. He traveled to the Soviet Union with André Gide in 1936 and later fought in the Spanish Civil War and was active in the Dutch Resistance, at times in hiding with Cas Emmer. Cas gave Keilson for his birthday a copy of Last's twenty-two-page book *Tao Ko Tao*, published illegally in 1944. The Chinese phrase means "The path to be taken is not the

More like songs than poems. He writes a kind of poetry that I don't like to read anymore. Pleasantly flowing along, too easily found, not concentrated enough—no work behind it. And you can tell. The first, "Child's Game," is well conceived. The others are so dithering. Just like he is—half eccentric, half artist, half blowhard. Perfunctory. That horrible poem about music! Which he was so proud of!

I believe, I do, I believe—but the moment I have to say what I believe in, I destroy my belief. So, my belief floats in thin air? Yes, it floats. In the air? Yes, it is light and invisible as air. And only when you don't have it and suffocate do you realize how necessary it is for life. I believe . . .

I know that Gertrud has fought a horrible struggle, which has left her very weak. She can't live withdrawn and inconspicuous like that, she has too much life force in her. She's too vital. Oh, if only she gets better. Is this what remains. I believe . . . Where do the dreams come from? Don't ask. Reason contradicts itself when it denies itself.—

A man being merely polite is often the greatest insult to the woman. He's just avoiding the fight, not treating

---

common path," and the poems are "marked by fierce, explicit Resistance in every word" (J. Cohen, *Onder de grond keimt de zaad* [*The Seed Grows Underground*]). The opening poem, "Child's Game," is about communication with God: "I play a child's game with God . . ."

her as an equal. That's something I've learned here. I often hope that the experience is only a threat—whose? who is threatening?—and advice for me: Be careful! I will be careful. Sometimes you have to change course from one day to the next. Not ironically/logically present proofs and arguments.

With Hanna briefly, who was very depressed and delicate. Hardly said a word. I tried to make her feel a little better. Only half succeeded. I hope I'll see her again tomorrow.

Arie is a great guy. Helped at once. Practical too. Superior to me in every way.

# *Sonnets*

Found among Hans Keilson's papers after his death in 2011 was a typescript of the following forty-six sonnets, initially misidentified as translations but eventually recognized by Keilson's editor Roland Spahr as the poems for Hanna Sanders. They were likely typed up while Keilson was still in Delft, but there is no evidence about the extent to which the order of poems in the manuscript matches the order in which they were written.

Keilson clearly intended them for publication at some point, but after the war he apparently did not try to publish them. Much later, he included three of the poems in his 1986 poetry collection *Sprachwurzellos* (a neologism that might be translated "Languagerootless" or "Uprooted/Unworded"), itself included in Keilson's collected works in 2005. These were Sonnets XII and XXVI in full and XLIV, about speaking in the enemy's German language, retitled "Fragment" and with lines 5–8 and 13–14 omitted, thus removing any reference to Hanna and her Dutch.

Given their autobiographical significance, the sonnets were published in the German edition of *1944*

*Diary*. Included here, they are the first translations of Keilson's poetry into English.

The poems are written in a clipped, tightly coiled German, making use of the language's grammatical markers to create a wrought, elliptical, intense style that requires a certain care and attention to unpack. Keilson maintains a strict meter and rhyme scheme throughout—almost all the sonnets follow the Shakespearean or Petrarchan pattern—often by eliding word endings, bending the rules of German word order, and occasionally using Dutch words instead of German (for example, *Heraut* instead of the German *Herold*, "herald," to rhyme with the German word *Braut*, "bride").

These translations are meant to be poetry, not prose, and I rhymed where I could, but I did let the documentary value of the poems, as the record of Hans and Hanna's relationship, take priority over alterations in content that might have better conveyed the form.

I son, you daughter, children of one blood,
so bitter ripe for Death in his fierce mowing,
deep in the darkness of our sorrow's courage
his poison brews a seed for a new sowing.

New sowing! As though for a time of peace,
love's voices leaving us no longer orphaned.
His eye has glimpsed us, nonetheless we shunned
his merciless pale hands circling without cease.

We bring, my darling, all of that with us
into our love's embraces: death, pale horror.
Not one kiss do we see except through tears,

and don't know, when we hear by night the screams
cry out from the earth: Is that a rondelay
it sings? Love being born, or grave's decay?

Tired of thinking, of fears that never end,
like nighttime eyes at broken windowpanes,
I sat at water's edge, while wild waves carried
the darkling rush of stars to the firmament.

And clouds of sighs that no wind could disperse
nor any prayer. My mouth of songs so cold!
I held a branch in my clenched hand and whipped
the water with a loveless savagery.

Behind me, I heard someone swing his switch
in time with me. I never knew who it was.
He stopped as soon as I raised my voice in song.

And when I paused, I heard him breathing hard.
And so we alternated, he and I.
I sang and wrestled with him as Jacob had.

III

Confess! Tell me your age, tell me your name!
Half child, half woman, already in the throes
of deepest currents. Coursing, your blood flows
as though sown with a love that does not find

its satisfaction in embraces. With
fulfillment comes new dreams, and new desires.
And soon your youth is wasted. The delusion
breaks, the fruit shrinks back into its seed.

And he who looks upon you, still unsure
whether to taste the fruit that's ripened now,
the waiting bud, has sacrificed all rest,

the peace sleep once obediently brought to him.
He stands at the window. Darkness here below.
A star flares up and vanishes in the night.

IV

When I bent closer, I could see in you
the dead man, still so strong and still unburied
beside the wall. The way the soldiers left
him lying there, he heavily lay in you.

His body filled the eye's whole background so
you couldn't see him, blinded as you were,
stunned by the fear that he no longer felt
once fallen victim to his life's last hour.

I hesitated. Can she be a lover
when she so sisterly is death's own bride?
My dead brother, is it your kiss alone
that glows from lips that languish there for me?

I took you by the hand, and then we two
as one, eye to eye, buried him in us.

V

So, is this love? Or friendship? Gaze and kiss
enough for us? Or are the heart's hot rays
cut to too sharp an edge? Or has he cast
his lot with worshipping the throne of genius?

Does every contact, deeper grasping, sear
a wound into affinity's pure crystal?
Does the onrushing of an ardor's glow
erupt within? Can acts of growing grow?

So close in distance, in its nearness so
far off, is this a pairing off without
a final self-renunciation? Out

pours like a heady ferment his whole sorrow
—oh lust, when it sees itself, so unashamed—
into our dialogue as yet unnamed.

VI

—Come now, sing! —I cannot sing. —One song?
—I don't know what. —Are you ashamed?
    —Perhaps
that too. But my heart radiates a sadness
when its own melody must remain unsung.

And anyone who's sad can only flee
from song. —But if it were to yield, someday,
to love? —Then, yes, it's possible, maybe
a song into my mouth would find its way . . .

And when you sang, with notes' dark quivering,
a foreign folk song like a common rite,
as though a swift baton in you were striking

up the rhythm to a lively dance,
I felt float up toward me from below
a breath of kisses and of tenderness.

My sister, crying all night long—I lay
beyond the wall and heard how brutally
her body's sobs betrayed her. She, the elder,
so very different, so full of hot pride,

not soft like me, I like to cry . . . Inside
her room I stood and all around me felt
the cries' dark buffeting, more violent
than any my own sore love had ever brought;

and at her bedside, as though for myself,
cried tears the whole night through for someone
   else,
one not in my own heart. I never cried

as bitterly as I did then. There was
no other way to console her, and me,
than to unite with her that night in tears.

VIII

I know your face when sad and when it laughs,
by day and when it dreaming silent broods.
Now too in sleep. You were given me anew
when I took you from the arms of night into

my own. Your eyes, they begged: Be gentle, then
fell silent. Now I know the force that guides
your life—while breast and hair and lips all strive
to reach the one power not yet brought to life.

And an amazement, woven 'tween the soul
and wonders upon wonders, now extends
between our eyelids, beneath the firmament,

gives our joint sleep so slowly burning shelter,
and rises from the tenderness of hand
in hand to the intimacy of Soon and Now.

IX

First you burned, a fire behind the mountain,
fueled to inferno by the valley's storm,
girded with fear, yet soon with smoke and shine.
It raged and broke through the soul's solid walls.

And then I burned, a pale glimmer under ashes
ere one forgets a red glow still remains.
The sparks increased, filling the shrine with
    treasure,
the way in poems word and word weave meshes.

Both of us within the sight of God
were blazing pillars of fire, day and night,
like Him when He spoke from a darkened cloud.

Generative breath of life, that brings
the work to completion. And then death, bright
    spirit
first shining when all acts of love are thought.

X

My first poem! It was written here, my love,
for you—you wrote it yourself inside me.
You are the mouth, while I am only she
in whom it carves love's signs like quill on paper.

The rise and fall of verses as they move—
your body's rhythm, gait, approaching me.
Rhyme on rhyme were first laid down in you.
I found them there, like mowings in the field.

And yet I cannot represent in words
how strong your arm is when it holds me tight,
until I melt in it and have no choice

but to let go; entirely soaked with you
I clamber down into the depths of dreams
and lose myself and you, O death, O world.

If I your mouth then you must be my breath,
driving the waves at night, beating on the beach.
I exhaled into you the wondrous gift
received from tenderly finding you in grief.

I burst in powerfully upon your life,
by guessing, recognizing, your young pain.
You stammered: Why do I feel this suffering?
I kissed you. That became, then, your first song.

Your first poem! It was born inside of you:
yours was the pain and yours the blessedness
of tears which now had lost their bitterness.

I felt how desperately your heart cried out—
but do not thank me anymore. You wear
the knight's gold spurs. So ride, until you're free!

XII

Your little room, walls mirrorless and bare
surrounding you, the fringe round your long
    waiting,
and we, together, hand in hand in hiding
sit behind the curtained window, stare

out sadly at the garden, where the blossoms
cradle the year in colors; from the hard
surrendered days it fell like healing balsam
on tired, stared-out eyes—and so returned

to us an image from the outside world
that strengthened the abandonment in us.
Your room grew, turned into a house, with doors

and windows; before long our friends had come
to visit. Only, Death notes down the guests,
then hunts them all down—one by one by one.

*A 2005 note on this poem says "Written in March 1944."*

## XIII

Break me again! Let none of me remain.
I am no longer good for anything.
Break my pride! Spare nothing, not a thing,
even if tears are forced out from the pain.

Everything in me that might serve you
as celebration now is yours. So take
it as a gift. Whether you'll let it go,
and what you've seized will ever come back to me . . .

I do not know. And even this not-knowing
is pleasure to me. What is it this hand
will make of me? A pillow to rest your head,

emblazoned with my suffering's gaudy band?
Or mighty weapon to win victory over
all obstacles? Is it a fatherland?

XIV

The first time that I saw her: She was standing
in the room as on fields bare with March,
as far from me as beating heart can push
one surge right to the edge until the next.

The threshold crossed, she offered me her hand;
I saw pain and confusion in her eyes.
I felt a major third leap from the scale's
first note, questioning, and binding us in a chord.

Later I asked her. She looked at her feet
—her dark hair falling over brow and face—
said nothing. But I pushed her, when exactly

was it that she knew for sure she loved me?
She thought it over. Then ran her fingers through
her hair and, breathing deep, pronounced these
    words:

*This sonnet was inserted before the following one in the manuscript, as a kind of
preface or prologue.*

XV

My childhood home, the last house on our street,
was mowed down like a field beneath the gashes
of the plow. The fifth day of the war
it was. So I would leave my youth in ashes.

Through smoking beams I spied my father's pale
and searching face. What once had borne the
     weight
of honest years of honest work and toil
lay suddenly destroyed in a few hours' hate.

But over there, amid the dusty wreckage
one single thing remained for us to find,
as though it still stood on our home's high ledge,

a candleholder, arms outspread—all seven.
I clambered to it and felt in my hand,
oppressive like the promise of glory: love.

*The Germans invaded the Netherlands on May 10, 1940; the Dutch resisted,
and on May 14, the German air force bombed Rotterdam, destroying the entire
center of the city.*

XVI

The first tender touches, desire unwounded,
caressing in the tips of fingers
a body's form, cool and rounded
in the swelling of limbs, lingers

along the gentler way to the center—
how lonely her consolation tastes,
her thirsting gutted by deeper fire
incurable, smoldering to new thirsts.

Lonely, too, the heart that once shared
drunken confidences together,
now returned from foreign expanses

alone, to its own beat that heals no wounds.
The way memory of a distant horror
yearns to feel its first tender touches.

XVII

Love holds depths of horror,
horror the weight of love.
If one's forgotten, the other
you'll never catch sight of.

Fathomless comprehension
strikes the poor heart blind.
Where love and horror grow as one
there dawns a fearsome light.

Branches of one tree,
like flowers on one stem,
grow in the Orphic sky

with no purpose or end.
Dream-in-dream their being,
drunken death and game.

XVIII [*written in the manuscript:* "(IX?)"]

Those hours of her life, time still her own—
she speaks to me of them in hours of love,
when she as her companion chooses me
at the fountain of joy to which her heartbeat flows:

I saw her as she was then, as a child,
a girl, in flower, tormented by longing
dreaming, hiding from herself her shame.
And yet a gentle stirring in her kiss.

She lay in my arms as if newly born,
forever young between the day and night
before the herald sun had time to rise.

Forgotten, wordlessly embraced as one
in pain's sharp glow. And then, when morning
   broke,
she rose up from the bed, beloved, bride.

Music to my ears! To eyes, the shape
of the love god when struck by his own arrow.
All those who cringe will feel his power rip
open the way to their senses, nuptially.

But those whose souls can offer no resistance,
in whom the arrow plunges deeper, they
are caught—most distant echo in the woods
of secrets, where the animals await.

A song in them then—even frightful terrors
can find the music calling forth the dance,
pushing the realm of the soul from highest corners

to a nameless sound. It tremblingly floats.
Then Pan is both: both love and the awaking
of darkest depths in which horror is quaking.

XX

"How dumb my mouth is, ever since your mouth
has taught with kisses other, deeper shudders.
Oh silence, of an animal's dull grief,
when inside, too, instincts cry out for relief.

It ripened slow within me; as a girl
laughter, lamentation gripped my soul.
What deadly silence that these songs resounded
with in festive wedding ceremonies."

"Do not be sad, love. In your silence speaks
the new song that our limbs together sing.
Like the fire of the sun, when day

breaks, sky earth water wrestling in heat,
so too your body speaks its own love call.
In soul the flesh, in flesh I find the soul."

## XXI

You came at evening, you left in the morning.
And in between the heart's own rhyme is found:
we found it for each other. Its secret homeland
is darkly hid in secrets of the blood

that flow together in the night. It bears
all sorrows; deep in its plasma lies the core:
that you are home with me and I with you—
from evening when you came until the morning.

Still, just as your coming proclaims the night,
just as your going announces day too soon,
our dialogue contains something unrhymed,

appearing unasked, that no pain can relieve.
He who finds rest in himself descends undaunted
the path that leads out into nothingness.

## XXII

Sometimes I am a stranger to my heart:
I feel it as another's strangely beating
rhythm of love. Tormenting doubt makes lips
less confident that they can bring a kiss

to another pair of lips, one bearing grief.
Oh fountain-mouth, dried up, arid and barren!
It is the ragged funeral shroud of love,
with which the soul, on loveless days, does sheath

itself. Its game has often in this rough
transforming suddenly torn into shreds
my precious image, then sunk down on cushions,

numb with pain. I will never get it back.
And then, alone, too late, it seemed I felt
a kiss upon my mouth, still warm with tears.

XXIII

Death is ordinary, like the glass
we drink from when we're thirsty. Then put down.
As everyday as that! With calloused hand
Death waves us over for a little fun.

Everyday too: with poison, treachery, gas
and fear of dying, of how it will go.
Finally he is the father who brings home
his child, the one who was for so long lost.

Horror is different, twisted as the eye
reflects what's in the background of its time
with dull defiance, like a whining child

who cannot play and cannot be consoled.
This horror has barred the path to death, remains
indomitably distant and withdrawn.

XXIV

I often think: When I am old and think
back to those days in which I loved and wrote you
poèm after poem, and, from your love,
a kiss alone remained, in memory true;

and when—the thought of mine goes on—alone,
I read with my old eyes what I then wrote,
and you, my love, give to me one last time
the gift of breath in which your heartbeat flowed,

then I can feel, today, the first gray hairs
and bitter wrinkles round my yearning mouth,
the gentle twilight stream of late remembrance

dissolving the particles of my mad lust.
Your soul, eternal, rises up in these moments
I spend torn loose from time and free of fears.

XXV

Time of horror, when we, as refugees,
fled toward love, when death proclaimed the hour
of the soul, and yet again was told to us
an ancient breviary's yellowed saying.

The heart's tree stood within the rich adornment
of early flowers, stood in the mouth of kisses.
How a body bent in my arms, so curved,
so intimate, still innocent in the lust

of young limbs. When in whispers the warm
    breath's
own wellspring trickled through the moss of
    slumber
and then melted away, oh, how it shuddered,

senses sharper in the lap of dreams.
That was the time of horror, which brought love.
That was the time of love, when horror waits.

The last word in the poem is wacht, which in German means "wakes, is
wakeful," but which here may be a Dutchism from wachter, "one who waits."
I follow the Dutch translator in choosing the latter reading.

XXVI

Come, sleep! Here your bed is made:
valerian blossoms, poppy's shade.
All the wild beasts silent fall.

Night wears its diadem of stars,
emblem of love's radiant glow.
Violins; harps; guitars.

Starlight drips down from the source;
the moon blows its horn of silver.
Coral beetles everywhere
glitter on mountains, valleys, rivers.

Bedded down gently as slumber's moss
in brain's and lap's warm beating.
The ferryman brings his skiff to harbor.
Come, sleep! Here is your midnight kiss.

XXVII

War and persecution: the melody
that the tune of our love moves along;
ardor and shuddering, firm like a prayer,
often near silence, the shepherd's reed pipe dying.

Screams like drumbeats lie within its song,
set above its deeper voices: Earth
turning round in the empty space of death
to horrors' litanies, rattling as it turns.

You, sounds, sweeping hollow through death's
    land—
we've heard your call, your voice for ages now,
even before your echoes, blended, shrill;

exiled and forlorn, until a shell
offered the ear your song, a crescendo comes,
and from the ground an answer rises up.

XXVIII

Deep conversations, weaving words
on golden threads in a heartfelt dance
of coupled natures, heads inclined
when thoughts to drunken talk advance—

We have often camped along
these rivers bright, our features clearer
in their reflection, where stream gushes
and lips grow wet in exchanging kisses.

At times the tide washed up deep silence
from the ground. It seeped into the heart.
A quiet unity, pure, resounded,

like a whirlpool drew into its spell
innermost dreams, and ardor, and shudder;
then, oh wonder, welcome and farewell.

## XXIX

Love nót just the friénd.
Learn too from the foe!
Before he has found
you awaits your woe.

All things in Nature
are shot from one bow.
Poisons and kieselgur
joined in you flow.

The way one hurls far
from the shore hook and bait,
throw yourself into time.

We gauge self from hate
that snaps where we suffer
and fight it: in the other.

"Kieselgur," also called "diatomaceous earth" or "diatomite," a soft rock easily
crumbled into powder, seems like merely a far-fetched rhyme for "Nature" (in
German: Natur / Kieselgur). In fact, it was one of the materials used to
stabilize hydrogen cyanide into Zyklon B, the poison gas used in the Holocaust.
Keilson seems to have heard such details even in 1944, perhaps through Leo
Rientsma, who was a chemist.

XXX

There are so many that one tear must serve
alone to grieve for siblings, parents, friends,
all who have suffered death, met horrible ends.
Oh graves, whoever seeks the traces of

your blood upon the meadowlands of woe
will stalk with hungry wolves, cheated of food,
into the desert, till, in a fit of madness,
he finds but skeletons and lemures.

For in the earth, lying deep, somewhere forgotten,
in rocks by sources of the wellsprings pure,
near old roots, in the heat of bygone sun,

witnesses kissed to sleep by the pale horror
rest fathomless and as incapable of
being known or grasped as is the joy of love.

*Lemures are frightening shades or restless spirits of the dead in Roman
mythology.*

## XXXI

As when a fiddler practices every day,
countless hundred times, tuning his bow
until it is the soul's own sounds that play
in and with the wood's defenseless echo,

when hand and soul are one—so too, beloved,
my mouth rehearsed in silence as your name rang,
the heart untiringly sending good word of it
surging up pure to lips, its joy in song.

And now whenever I, in bitter night,
lie sleepless, thinking, whispering into space
the name's sweet sound—when I of you have
    thought,

wand'ring the path of night on its narrow seam,
it sounds to me, awake and trembling, echo,
consoling dark bell tone of ore and dream.

## XXXII

"Woe unto those who sing the songs of love!"
It is the lie that stamps the sweetest words
with seals of misery. Only horror, heard
from our mouths speaking as though poisoned,
   gives

off an abyss's thick smoke. Then bitter shame
compels us. Who can unmask love? Who bears
the loathing nurtured by the God of Death:
woe unto those who sing the songs of love . . . ?

Yet like an alchemist, seeking precious metal
in transformation from a lesser ore,
melting it down within the crucible,

imagining awful spells drawn from a star—
so too your being has, in a magic stroke,
reminted the word beneath whose weight I'd sunk.

XXXIII

Your eye has tears, and kisses has your mouth,
your hands caresses, and your hair a shine—
that's how I see you now, your image shown
in the abandon of its movements. Wreathed

in light the ceremonial festival
when you held me and put your arms around
me like a ring, and when our sacred bond
unveiled its signet. Kiss and dance are all

that stay in memory, deep recollection
of what we shared; there is no other way,
no escape in any other direction

to other fates, only perfect completion,
obedience to Eros, and oblivion
in carefree love until the final dawn.

Darkness—you and I, the furtive pair,
blind enraptured guest of moonless night,
city and countryside almost asleep,
and up above us, with dark wafted hair,

clouds chasing clouds in this their year of storm.
Soft and lightly measured was your pace,
holding me close to you, tight in your arm,
happy to walk like this. And yet your face

so ghostly, spectral, as if in a dream.
Then shots rang out. There're fighter planes tonight.
Into the sky's dark dome stretched arms of light.

Then a deep shaking rumbled in the ground.
You stood . . . I saw it. And I calmed your fear,
with one kiss, as with it I brought love near.

XXXV

Take lies and art, disguise and vanity,
take all well-wrought delusion from a man,
from word and deed! And push him off his course
of cold pride, then he will court helplessly—

Take everything from him the way he takes
your dress off to see you bare, let him come close
to you, pathetic, naked . . . And then ask:
What's left now of your pluck and sneers and jokes?

Take the lies, and I will still have art.
Take the art, my pride's worth all the more.
And without pride, so dear to me?—One last

delusion still remains, precious, carefree:
My life remains to me, in tears it sees
its own example, when love's morning comes.

XXXVI

A day of remembrance! When the memories
of deeds, of people from departed years,
creep up over the heart; when precious loved ones
rise up in the mind to turns of fate

And speak to us in the tongue of the dead—
Oh insubstantial hordes, long since grown ancient,
what sweet and musty smell in your clothes and
     hair,
what soft breath from the grave to pain and
     twilight.

Old expired agonies—peace and prayer.
Flood of tears—like frozen-over streams,
and like fish in them, lifeless: grief and fear.

And falsity, and crime—too late, too late!
Only love's flowered pasture, white with snow,
beneath which it coos and whispers, blind and
     warm.

## XXXVII

Gas! Sweeter than any gas,
so light in structure and in weight,
into you as into a vase
death exhales its face:

brow and mouth and nose.
Painless as opium,
your seed fills the lungs and blood
of rotting carrion.

Bodies, jammed into chambers,
so credulous of opening taps:
in slowly strangling cries

out of the last delusion you've snapped
when harder than the blows of hammers
wafts overhead the flag of horror.

## XXXVIII

When lordly reason ordered me: Do this!
I disobeyed. I did, nonsensically,
what ripened in the heart's simplicity.
Concealed divinity points the way to things

that lie beside the way; it augurs pain.
No boastful thinking can cheat soul and world.
The smell of flowers, honey sweet unfurled—
I found it hid in deepest dungeon, lain

in love's foreboding. —So too, my beloved,
I saw your image when my beating heart
blazed a trail across its bounds to you,

where all that was confused was clarified
in blissful act, when I succumbed, and peace
was banished from my mind as you came near.

XXXIX

Immortal poèms, men and women from
a bygone age, we read you so entranced—
like over meadows, through our lips you've come
in timeless stride, till reaching deepest horror:

in our day too your melody is heard,
talismanic even in fury of war.
Your splendid body rises up high over
atrocities and graves, speaking its word

never more beautifully than in love's tongue
of mortal hearts that God has lit afire.
What splendor, what a blessing on fallow ground

of pale existence poured into us then:
when bombs were dropped on London and on
    Wien—
Shakespeare, Verlaine, Rossetti, Hölderlin!

*Wien is the German name for Vienna, pronounced "Veen" and rhyming with "Hölderlin."*

XL

Look, this is our enemy: he who took
the act to its outermost limit and then leapt
across that line and, full of reckless lies,
strew dragon's seeds of disaster at the skies.

Look at his face: is't not a mask or shell,
over great deeds but with a lying shape?
What's large looks small—what's noble turns
     to deep
disgrace in his blind, vile, and selfish will.

We are his, and so too he is ours.
We are as dreadful in his horror hand
as he in that of one who never forgets

that anyone who stands in mortal form
and hoists his flags of victory premature
becomes a dreadful curse, self-exiled, banned.

*The first half of line 9,* "Wir sind die Seinen," *is a reference to the final poem
in Rilke's* Book of Images: "Death is large. / We are his, / mouth laughing. /
When we feel in the midst of life, / he ventures to weep / in the midst of us."

Immortality! Does love mean: Never
die? Was ever doer like finished deed?
And does the deed fall victim to decay
like a guilt one asks for with a shudder?

Late in the year, when happily the heart
presses the tart intoxicated wine,
it is as if the glass contains a sign
foreboding the shards to come when the drinker
    breaks it.

To love is to be mortal and to move
within the circle of change, rise burn and fall,
the memory of a distant melody

of being, guiltless in struggles of inaction,
a homecoming in tears from the sore journey
which one set out on bold and still unvanquished.

XLII

Just one melody, immortal,
a single immortal song!
before your pleas fled from my mouth,
your mouth evaded my kisses.

Immortal! If for once I sing
what sounded first so pure in you,
and then, like steely blade, I raise
up songs of sacrifice.

The earth, it gave the body dust,
water gave tears to eyes,
fire sun's sustaining O,

the sky the feeling breeze.
You passed the time in tying
and tightening the string on the bow.

When does love end? When does the time of horror
subside on the bare shore of deserted senses?
When does the wind erase from the dull sand
fissures of waves' play at which seagulls cried?

Spray still wets the cliffs and breakers crash
round house and tower. From ramparts it shines,
a promise made to us, here shuddering,
of the night port of its immensity.

At first is praise, the end procures rebukes;
the clock of destiny no longer wants to toll.
Its noble workings, gear and spring and wheel,

interlocked with itself and never dying.
Love never ends. The horror's circling hand
shows hours, minutes, of only eternity.

XLIV

Has any poet ever grudged the tongue
he speaks as I do mine? My bitter shame
at having taken signs and syllables
defiled by the rabble from its very mouth?

And doubly grudged, since she who sings my song—
you, love, one both the child of foreign tongue
and kin to me, whom the same threats surround—
you brood as on your own upon my sounds.

And every word that all but unwillingly
slips out of me and stands there, just reminds me
of what I've damned, and heavy grows the burden

of my poems, hard in a mouth like stone.
You, loving-rasping, speak their rhythm and sound,
gave them shine and ring anew, so I could forget.

*A 2005 note on this poem says "Written in December 1944."*

When your eyes, dark and brown, reflect in them
the course and flight of deeper thoughts, proclaim
more than your mouth can answer to my hundred
questions, tell and tell and never enough—

I see at once, in its earliest stirrings, what
moves you, what dawns so tenderly inside,
and seem to see a spirit carriage drive
out from your eyes' depths, carrying your gaze.

But often, a pale ray, reflected in
the wet of tears, shines down from the clenched
   horror
of your inner gaze into a realm of love.

It fills the bowl to overflowing. Then
a wasteland, ragged grass, comes into view . . .
Upon it, blind, rambling, alone, is you.

XLVI

Some things in years past that I've done now come
back to me different, not as what they were.
They summon up before my eyes a creature
as he was then, when these acts were his own.

And, mirror mirroring mirror, the long line
of deeds done propagates. The doer, I,
stand silently, with no shame or regret,
as though all gave off boundless fealty.

But you, mirror, without mist on the glass
from the purest breath, in which I see myself,
you unite all these deeds under the seal

that your love stamps in wax as pledge and pawn.
You carry the last brick to the house of life
where the fugitive will stay, he whom love ties.

# *Afterword*

With Arie Bakker's help, Keilson returned to Gertrud and to Naarden. And there he stayed, in hiding until Germany's surrender in May 1945 and openly thereafter. Hans and Gertrud were married soon after the end of the war and remained together in Naarden, then in nearby Bussum, until Gertrud's sudden death in 1969. Hans lived in Bussum until his death in 2011, practicing psychoanalysis well into his nineties. I met him the day before his hundredth birthday.*

His novel written in 1944, *Comedy in a Minor Key*, was published in 1947, the same year as the Dutch edition translated by "H. Sanders." The novel is dedicated "For Leo and Suus in Delft." Of the other novels he began in hiding, he would finish only *The Death of the Enemy* (see 10/24, p. 87), published as *The Death of the Adversary* in 1959. Along with the early *Life Goes On*, Keilson's fourth and only other work of fiction was a short story, "The Dissonance Quartet," commissioned in 1968 for

* Described in my essay "Man of the Century," *The Believer* (Sept. 2010; also available online).

a German anthology on fathers and sons.* He felt that he no longer had a literary audience and decided for good to be a doctor, not a writer.

He also never forgot the words of his late father from their final meeting: "Don't forget: You are a doctor!" After his parents' deportation, Hans never heard from them again.

From 1945 until 1970, Keilson worked as a psychiatrist with L'Ezrat Ha-Yeled (Children's Aid), the first organization founded for the care and treatment of Jewish orphans who had survived the Holocaust. He would eventually work with 204 of the barely 2,000 Dutch Jewish children who survived the war. In 1979, Keilson received the doctorate he was denied forty-five years earlier in 1934, with his dissertation, *Sequential Traumatization in Children*, becoming the standard work in the field; it was translated into English in 1992. Keilson himself says that the dozens of case histories of Dutch Jewish children in the dissertation are his late literary work—little nonfiction short stories of Jewish fates—and that his dissertation was his way of "finally saying Kaddish, the prayer for the dead, which I had

* *Comedy in a Minor Key*, tr. Damion Searls (FSG, 2010); *The Death of the Adversary*, tr. Ivo Jarosy (1962; FSG 2010); *Life Goes On*, tr. Damion Searls (FSG, 2012); "The Dissonance Quartet," tr. Damion Searls, in the *Forward* (2017).

been unable to say for so long." He was at least as proud of his psychological work as he was of his fiction.

Appalled at the silence of the Catholic Church during the Holocaust, Gertrud converted to Judaism after the war; she also remained firmly opposed to returning to Germany. Hans later said that it was because of her that he stayed in Holland; he also said, in a 2010 interview, "When I heard my parents had died, I stopped being a German." But he did not hate the Germans. The reason he did not return to his homeland was: "I knew I wouldn't be able to practice in Germany. I couldn't have helped but make the Germans feel guilty about me, because they were Germans and I was a Jew, so there was no way I could be a therapist for Germans in Germany."

Hans and Hanna stayed briefly in contact, and while he worked for L'Ezrat Ha-Yeled, Hanna worked for the government organization responsible for those same children. Hanna was impressed with Gertrud when they finally met, and apparently translated some of her handwriting-analysis reports for work. In 1946, Hanna married Chanan Hoffman, a German Jew from Hamburg who had fought in the Jewish Brigade and emigrated to Palestine. She sent a short letter to Keilson after his remarriage to Marita Lauritz in 1970, which he kept and treasured; they may have met once more, in the 1980s, when Hanna and Chanan visited the Netherlands.

Hanna died in 2008, at age eighty-five, having never

spoken about her time in hiding except in a short interview, in Hebrew, for the Ghetto Fighters' House Archives in 1989, in which she expressed enormous gratitude to Arie and Evy Bakker. It was in 2010 that Marita found Hans Keilson's diary in a drawer, deciphered and read parts of it to him, and learned what it was—and first heard about Hanna. An editor discovered the sonnets in Hans's papers after his death in 2011, at age 101.

Hanna's two children do not know German or Dutch; when Marita Keilson contacted them about the rediscovered *1944 Diary*, they had never heard of Keilson or the novel of his that their mother had translated. Marita sent them the English translation of *Comedy in a Minor Key*, from which they learned more about life in hiding than Hanna had ever told them; when Marita gently broached the topic of Hans and Hanna's affair, they responded: "We are actually happy to find out that Hanna had a love affair in the middle of this hellish period." My translation of Sonnet XXIV, which Marita asked me to make for Hanna's son, Yoram Hoffman, in 2014, was the first piece of Hans Keilson's writing to and for Hanna that they were able to read.

In her forewords to the German and Dutch editions, Marita Keilson thanks "those who helped Hans to survive: Leo and Suus, Arie and Evy, Gertrud and Hanna," along with the generation that helped in various ways with the publication of the diary: Leo and Suus's children, Hannie Rientsma and Lies De Boer-Rientsma; Hanna's children, Yoram and Vardit Hoffman; Keilson's children, Barbara and Bloeme (Hans's daughter with Marita); and Bloeme's children, Leila and, born in 2009, another Hannah. I would like to thank these seven pairs here as well, plus an eighth—Marita Keilson and Roland Spahr, the editor who recognized the manuscript of sonnets.

## A Note About the Author

Hans Keilson is the author of *Life Goes On*, *Comedy in a Minor Key*, and *The Death of the Adversary*. Born in Germany in 1909, he published his first novel in 1933. During World War II he joined the Dutch resistance. Later, as a psychotherapist, he did pioneering work with children who had suffered war trauma. He died in 2011 at the age of 101.

## A Note About the Translator

Damion Searls is the author of three books and the translator of thirty books from the German, French, Norwegian, and Dutch. He rediscovered the work of Hans Keilson; his 2010 translation of *Comedy in a Minor Key*, published to international acclaim when Keilson was one hundred years old, was a *New York Times* Notable Book and a National Book Critics Circle Award finalist.